CW00522142

Big Jim

Jim Mills – A Rugby

*Best Wish
Jim Mills*

Peter Lush and Maurice Bamford

London League Publications Ltd

Big Jim
Jim Mills – A Rugby Giant

© Peter Lush and Maurice Bamford.
Foreword © Doug Laughton.

The moral right of Peter Lush and Maurice Bamford to be identified as the authors has been asserted.

Cover design © Stephen McCarthy.

Front cover: Jim in action for Wales against Australia at Swansea in 1975 in the World Championship.
Back cover photo: Widnes in September 1979 with the Challenge Cup, John Player Trophy, BBC2 Floodlit Trophy and the Lancashire Cup (Aaron Photography); Jim scoring at Wembley in the 1975 Challenge Cup Final.

All photographs in this book are from private collections unless otherwise credited. No copyright has been intentionally breached; please contact London League Publications Ltd if you believe there has been a breach of copyright.

A CIP catalogue record for this book is available from the British Library.

Second (paperback) edition with minor changes from the first hardback edition published in Great Britain in November 2013 by:
London League Publications Ltd, P.O. Box 65784, London NW2 9NS

ISBN: 978-1-909885-01-1

Cover design by: Stephen McCarthy Graphic Design
                               46, Clarence Road, London N15 5BB

Layout: Peter Lush

Printed & bound in Great Britain by CPI Group (UK) Ltd, Croydon CR0 4YY

Jim Mills's share of the profits from this book will be donated to the Widnes & Runcorn Cancer Support Group.

Foreword

I first met 'Big Jim' when he signed for Widnes. We were weight training in groups in stations and I was bench pressing 190 pounds. Jim picked up the bar and curls, the hardest lift. He was curling 190 pounds as if they were toffee hammers. After an age he asked me "What do I do next?" I replied "Start another group on your own about 100 yards further down the gym." We were in a state of shock.

As a rugby player Jim was a huge, very fit, fast, intelligent, tough forward who I never saw take a backward step. You would want Jim in your team anywhere, anytime. In all the years I played with and against Jim I never saw him bully or strike first at a lesser opponent. I have seen him sort it out if anyone attacked one of our team.

When tackle counts came into our game I was assistant coach to Frank Myler. One day Frank said to me: "Doug, big Jim has only done one tackle all game." I said to Frank: "Have a word with him," and Frank did. "Jim, you only made one tackle in all the game, what have you got to say?" Looking him straight in the eye, Jim said: "Frank would you run at me during a game?" The team meeting ended in laughter as nobody in their right mind would run near big Jim.

Once we played Barrow at Naughton Park. It was scorching hot; the temperature was in the 90s. They kicked off; I caught the ball and skipped through. Jim was alongside me and ran 70 yards to score under the posts. Prior to them kicking off I turned to Jim, who was still panting and said "Same again Jim." "Be off with you" came the reply...

On the 1979 Lions tour to Australia, before going to bed he would pick up a mini-car on the dual carriageway and turn it round the other way. He would say "I bet that fellow wonders what's going on." I would reply "I bet you he knows".

Jim was my assistant coach for a while, and went on to be chairman at Widnes. Previously he was on the committee, and two directors nearly came to blows. Jim had to hold them apart.

Jim and I went to sign Jonathan Davies, who was, and still is, the biggest signing in rugby league. I had been on sales training courses and told Jim "Whatever you do, when I go for the decision I will rub my nose; don't speak. Jonathan must be the next to speak." Afterwards, Jim said "You must have been silent for ages". "No, it was one minute, 20 seconds" I told him. I timed it.

I was his best man at his wedding; I am godfather to his son and remain a great friend to this day.

Doug Laughton
Newton-le-Willows
April 2013

Introduction

Anybody interested in the traditions of Rugby League Football before Super League must surely know of the great character and tremendous club and international forward, Jim Mills. For many seasons, both here and in Australia, Jim Mills strode like a Colossus around the muddy grounds of this country in winter and Sydney's bone hard playing surfaces in the much warmer environs of the antipodes. At six feet four inches tall and of heavyweight proportions, Jim was a very tough and forthright forward. No one took liberties with Jim or any of his team mates and he was very highly respected in a sport that had more than its share of extremely hard characters. Jim's career was surrounded by success, controversy and humour.

The success centred around his international caps for Wales and for Great Britain. He made two Lions tours in 1974 and 1979 and could have made it three, having been chosen to tour in 1970, but he opted to play in Australia for North Sydney. He played in three Challenge Cup finals, four Lancashire Cup finals and three John Player finals, a BBC2 Floodlit Trophy final and a Premiership Final.

The controversial aspect of his game was that which sometimes surrounds big, tough forwards in that it was – according to some spectators and referees – always Jim's fault when fights erupted even though he may have been 10 yards away from the incident. Jim was sent off 20 times in his more than stormy career, some deserved, some not. But the incident mostly remembered was in 1975 when Jim was playing for Wales in the 1975 World Championship. Jim was involved in an incident with the giant New Zealand forward, John Greengrass, which left the Kiwi severely injured. So incensed were the New Zealand authorities that they refused to play against Jim ever again.

The humorous side of Jim's career is emphasised by the many tales about him, which his former team mates and opponents swear are all true. For years now, after dinner speakers on the rugby league and union circuits have used Jim Mills's stories. Jim himself is an accomplished speaker and, in full flow, is hilarious. He explains his 20 dismissals by saying that "17 of them were mistaken identity". His warm personality makes him excellent company and he is never without a tale about the game he loves so deeply. The rich stories he has deserve to be told alongside the path of his glittering career and this biography is written to relate both his prowess as a great rugby league player, along with the humour that accompanies this living legend. So sit back and enjoy the story of the one and only Jim Mills.

Maurice Bamford
April 2013

Preface

Working with Jim on this book has been a fascinating experience. I never saw him play – I started watching rugby league at Fulham, and saw my first live game in October 1980, by which time Jim had retired. As part of the research for this book, I watched the DVD of the 1978 'Dad's Army' test. Sadly, the 1975 Challenge Cup Final, one of Jim's most memorable games, is not available on DVD.

The significance of that game was not apparent at the time. The Australians were clearly a good side, but apart from losing that test, were beaten by Warrington, and as Jim proudly recalls, Widnes. No one at Odsal that day would have thought it would be 10 long years until Great Britain beat the Australians again, and how much their game would have progressed when the next tourists, the magnificent 1982 side, arrived.

What it did confirm for me was how much the game has changed. Both teams took kicks at goal early on in the match from penalties; which if they did that today in a club match would have the other team's fans derisorily singing *Swing Low, Sweet Chariots;* implying that they should be playing rugby union. The game looked slower, but that partly may be because of the changes in the television coverage, which to someone used to watching Super League on Sky Sports, seemed very basic indeed. There was some enterprising play from both sides, and it should be remembered as an historic win for Great Britain. What it did re-enforce for me was that Jim played in a very different era, something confirmed by many of the past players we interviewed for this book.

One of the problems with an 'authorised' biography is that it can be too uncritical of the person the book is about. Jim undoubtedly was a very good rugby league player, with a remarkable try-scoring record in an era where scores were far lower than they are today. But there was also Jim's disciplinary record to consider. I wrote the *Count to three* chapter, and remember going to see Jim and giving it to him to read. We sat in his kitchen while he went through it; including the detailed analysis of his disciplinary record. "Fair enough" he said in the end, and I think we have dealt even-handedly fairly with the issues which arose in that part of Jim's career.

An interesting part of that research was trying to establish his sendings-off in Australia. Thanks to Australian rugby league historian David Middleton we finally got to an accurate record on this. This did produce one lighter moment. We used to meet to do the interviews in Jim and Ruth's kitchen. We were discussing Australia one day and Jim said, with some relief, "That's good; maybe I was only sent off three times in Australia". Ruth burst out laughing at this. But after all, it was an improvement on the often alleged five sendings-off.

There were many other interesting areas to explore. Jim's rugby union career is covered in detail in the book. To have established himself in the Cardiff first-team pack at the age of 20 was a remarkable achievement, given that union forwards often do not reach their peak until their mid- to late-20s. Who can tell how his union career would have developed had he not gone to Halifax? Had he continued to develop as a player, there is little doubt in my mind that he would have won Welsh caps, and been in contention for the British Lions.

Another very important part of Jim's identity is his Welsh roots. Despite having lived in the north of England since 1964, apart from his time playing for North Sydney, his support for Wales in the sporting arena and in other ways remains strong, and many of his friends in rugby league are former Welsh players.

Jim was involved in controversy during his career, some of which was not of his making. His return from North Sydney to sign for Widnes in 1972 caused problems that were still reverberating internationally in 1975, and prevented him from having a short-term playing stint in Sydney then. When that was finally resolved by the RFL, a few months later he was threatening court action against them when his ban for the John Greengrass incident was hugely increased on an appeal by Widnes against the ban. And he was drawn in, as Widnes chairman, to the controversy about the setting up of Super League, and which would clubs would be members of the initial competition.

So I hope this book is a fair account of Jim's career. Doing the research, I would come across a story on the internet, or from a former team-mate about Jim. I would ring him up, and ask "Is this really true?" Often they were, but some had grown a bit in the telling, and we have included them in the book as Jim remembered them. So next time you see a prop forward not sent off when all the fans feel he should have been; do wonder if he's given the referee a lift to the game, or persuaded the referee that he can't be sent off because he's the captain. Or maybe such things don't happen in modern day rugby league?

Enjoy the book; it was certainly enjoyable to work on it with one of the most pleasant and entertaining people in rugby league; as long as you didn't have to face him in the front row!

Peter Lush
July 2013

Memories of Cardiff Youth

I first met Jim Mills in the summer of 1961. We joined the Cardiff Youth team together where we had an unbeaten season, but more importantly friendships were formed that remain to this day.

Three things have always stood out for me with Jim Mills: his sense of humour, his commitment to playing and his right hook!

Our end of season tour took us to Weston-Super-Mare where, after soundly beating the opposing team we took a visit to the local dance hall, and with Robo and others at our side, it turned out to be a re-run of the gun fight at the OK Corral. Needless to say, along with everyone else, Jim's right hook was in good working order.

The sadness for me is that we only had one season together because Jim was a Welsh international and a British Lion in waiting, but he went north to an amazingly successful career which left his friends in South Wales very proud of his achievements.

There is only one Jim Mills and I'm very proud to be his friend.

Peter Thomas CBE

Peter Thomas CBE played for the Cardiff Youth team with Jim and is now the chairman and benefactor of Cardiff Blues. He is also a successful businessman in Wales and the United Kingdom, and has done a great deal to support rugby union.

Thank you

First of all to Jim, who has been interviewed numerous times, and answered many further questions by email.

To Ruth for her hospitality and contributions to the book.

To everyone who was interviewed for the book or wrote pieces for it; their recollections added a great deal to it.

To Phil Fearnley for providing access to an interview he did with Jim on *Halton Community Radio* 92.3FM.

To Robert Gate and David Middleton for assistance with statistics and other information.

To all photographers who provided photos for the book. All photos are from private collections unless otherwise credited.

To Steve McCarthy for his design work on the cover, and to the staff of CPI Antony Rowe for printing the paperback edition.

About this book

The initial work on this book was done by Maurice Bamford. After completing the first draft, Maurice then became ill, and had to give up writing for a period. We are pleased to say that at the time of writing he is making a good recovery. So Peter Lush then became involved, and did further research and interviews with Jim to complete the book.

About the authors

Peter Lush grew up in London, where he still lives. He has been watching rugby league since he went to a game at Fulham in October 1980 with Dave Farrar. In 1995, with Michael O'Hare, they wrote *Touch and Go – A history of professional rugby league in London*, and set up London League Publications Ltd. The company has now published almost 80 books, mainly on rugby league. Peter often has to work on book development and design, but books he has written or edited include *I wouldn't start from here, Tries in the Valleys, From Fulham to Wembley, The Rugby League Grounds Guide, Rugby League Review 2007, Rugby League Review Number 2,* (all with Dave Farrar), *Trevor Foster* (with Simon Foster and Robert Gate) *Peter Fox* (with Graham Williams), *Hendon Football Club* (with David Ballheimer) and two cricket grounds guides. He was also joint editor of *Our Game*, and has written for various magazines, journals and newspapers on the game. In real life he is the director of Training Link, a charity providing basic skills training to help people find work, in central London.

Maurice Bamford grew up in Leeds, and played professional rugby league for Dewsbury and Hull in the 1950s and early 1960s. After also playing in amateur rugby league, he turned to coaching. He had a distinguished career in coaching, including being the Great Britain coach for two years, from October 1984 to December 1986. He also coached Wigan, Leeds, Halifax, Huddersfield, Workington, Dewsbury, Bramley, Prescot, York, Keighley and Lancashire Lynx as well as various amateur clubs. Since retiring from coaching he has developed a new career in writing, and has written regularly for *League Weekly* and *Rugby League Journal*. He has written 12 books, including his *Memoirs*, biographies of Frank Myler, Vince Karalius, Arthur Clues, Kevin Ashcroft and Jeff Grayshon, and with London League Publications Ltd *Play to Win* and *Hunslet through and through*, a biography of Geoff Gunney. He lives with his wife Rita in Morley.

Contents

This book is dedicated by Jim to:

"My daughter Julie, a beautiful and brave girl, who will live on in our hearts for ever."

1. Starting out: Cardiff rugby union

Jim Mills was born on 24 September 1944 in the village of Cwmbach. The village is in the Cynon Valley, and grew during the nineteenth century as coal mining developed. The name means 'Little Valley'. The last pit closed in 1922, and the village declined because there was less work in the area. Today it has a population of just over 4,000. It is east of Aberdare, north of Mountain Ash and south of Merthyr Tydfil.

His dad, Jim Mills senior, was a boilermaker and served his apprenticeship in the railway steam sheds in Caerphilly, where he worked on the big steam locomotives. Jim's mother, Margaret who had been Margaret Thomas before she got married, had two sons, David and Jim.

A tall lad, Jim took after his father's side of the family who were all big, strong men. His granddad Bill Mills was six feet four inches tall. Bill had two brothers, Jack and Jim, who were even bigger than him. They worked as coal trimmers, spreading and grading the coal with shovels to level out the huge piles. This gave them superb physiques. Jack played rugby union in the second row for Cardiff. They worked in the Cardiff and Barry docks where the coal was tipped into the ships and the Mills boys spread it out for balance at sea. On his mother's side, Jim's grandfather was David John Thomas. He was a coal miner at Aberaman pit, and died at the pit, although not in a mining accident. Jim thinks he was around 50 years old. Aberaman is a village near Aberdare, the Colliery closed around 1955.

The Mills family had grown up in the Newtown area of Cardiff. Newtown was a small area between Cardiff Docks, Splott and the London to Swansea railway. It was built in the 1840s and provided homes for people working in the docks until the area was cleared in the late 1960s.

When Jim was around three years old, the family moved to the Ely area of Cardiff for his dad's work in the steelworks. Jim's dad played rugby union at school, and was a useful second rower. Jim recalls that "My dad didn't play rugby union after leaving school. He did play for a works team at the steelworks where he worked. He once played against Len Olsen, who later signed for Halifax."

As Jim grew up he was tall and began to fill out. He attended three different schools in the Ely area, Cwrt-yr-ala Junior School, at first, then

Class at Cyntwell School in 1957–58, Jim aged 13.

Windsor Clive and finally Cyntwell School. In his early years at Cwrt-yr-Ala Jim was a good goalkeeper for his school football team and made the final trials for the Cardiff Schools team. The headmaster was a former Cardiff rugby union player, Duncan Brown. He played for the club in 1931–32, and then from 1934–35 until 1939. He was a full-back, made 93 first team appearances and played in a final Welsh trial for the national team. After retiring as a player, he served on the club's Rugby Football Committee. However, the school only played football. Jim recalls: "I did not know that Duncan was involved in rugby in those days, but I remember him looking at me with pride when I played for Cardiff years later."

However, the geography teacher at Windsor Clive was Sid Judd, who played rugby union at flanker for Cardiff. He also won 10 caps for Wales, and scored one of the tries when they beat the All Blacks in 1953, and played for Cardiff when they beat the All Blacks on the same tour, also scoring a try. He died in 1959, aged 30, from Leukaemia.

He saw a fine potential second-rower in the 13-year-old Jim Mills. Jim recalls: "Sid Judd pulled me aside one day and said 'You don't want to be wasting your time playing soccer. Start playing rugby football, it will do you good', so I said OK and took to the game like a fish to water. I remember he said to me 'Here young Mills, if you go to the fish shop for me I will recommend you for a Cardiff schoolboys trial'.

Two years later he did and at the trials was a very fast young threequarter called Clive Sullivan, who went on to captain the Great Britain rugby league side. Clive and I made the Cardiff schools team.

He used to call me 'lanky' because I was like a bean pole in those days. Much later, when Clive was playing for Hull FC, I nailed him in a tackle good and hard and as we sprawled on the ground with him in a dazed condition, I said 'How's that for someone so lanky?' We both had a good laugh as we got up from the tackle."

Clive was a great pal of Jim's. They played together in Cardiff, then at rugby league for Wales and Great Britain and against one another for their clubs.

Another good player who made the grade at those trials was Ron Hill, who later went north to play for Castleford and Salford. Hill was in the Cardiff Schoolboys team with Jim when they won the Dewar Shield. Two other players Jim remembers from those days are Bertie Collins, Bernard Foster, Fred Phillips and David Ivins. Another player who Jim played with 'up north' was Dennis Brown: "He was at Widnes when I signed for them. We shared the same digs in Widnes, provided by Jean and Barry Hynan who looked after us very well. Dennis was in the Marines and would travel up to Widnes from Plymouth. We were chatting one day and found out that we had the same birthday."

Jim has many good memories of people from his schooldays: "Some good mates I remember from then include Terry James, George James, David Hicks – who a worked on the farm with after leaving school – also Murray David, and many good friends who I grew up with, Peter and Pat Collins, David Collins, Tony Collins and Tim Collins who were all brothers of Bertie Collins who played rugby with me in the Cardiff Schoolboys side, and their sisters Maureen and Mary Collins. Peter and Pat always make me very welcome when I visit them.

Their cousin Tommy Aitken is also a good friend of mine. Paul Healy, Brian Connelly, Tony Donovan, Peter Reed and Peter Tresize are all people I remember from that time. Although I have no immediate family in Wales, I still go down to Cardiff where I have many cousins on my father's side and many cousins in Aberdare on my mother's side.

When I was playing with Cardiff I always enjoyed going to Tiger Bay to the CIACs [Cardiff International Athletics Club], the entrance to which was under the railway bridge in Bute Street. Some wonderful characters and sportsmen came into the club and they had a good rugby team. Some great rugby league players played there in their youth including Billy Boston, Johnnie Freeman, Colin Dixon and David Willicombe. Another great player from Tiger Bay was Gus Risman.

When the West Indies cricket team was in Cardiff they always headed for the CIACs club, enjoyed a game of cards with the locals and had West Indian meals made for them. Great cricketers such as Gary Sobers, Wes Hall, Charlie Griffiths, Clive Walcott and Frank Worrall would all be there; it was always a good night at the club and I used to enjoy it. Local characters I remember from those days were Stretch Williams, Arthur Duarte, Roy and Peter Phillips, Sammy John, Alec Niel, Harry Ernest, Danny James, Billy's brother, Herbie Boston and many more. Also there was the former British Heavyweight Champion Joe Erskine who was Johnny Freeman's cousin."

When he left school Jim worked at Lower House farm at Michaelston-le-Pit, near Dinas Powis, which was near home. Jim recalls: "My mate, Dave Hicks and I would cycle the seven miles to the farm each day for a very early start work a long, hard day, six and a half days per week. Dave was a good mate and we worked well together.

Clockwise from top left: Jim aged 14; David and Jim with their Mum on holiday in 1960; Jim with his Mum & Dad on holiday in Porthcawl in the late 1950s; David with his Mum and Dad on holiday.

I had Saturday afternoons off to play my rugby and I would work Dave's shift for him on Sunday afternoons in lieu of me having time off to play. My main job was milking the cows, Jersey's and Friesians. I rounded up the cows into the shed about 6am, set up the milking, finished that job, moved the cows outside again, and cleaned out the shed. I'd then round them up again at about 5pm, milk them, let them out again, clean the shed and go home. I worked on the farm for two years and it helped me develop physically which was important for my rugby. When we were haymaking in the summer, my friend from Ely, Eddie Avoth, came to help us. Eddie later became the British and Commonwealth Light Heavyweight boxing champion."

Jim has always had a keen interest in boxing: "Besides rugby I love the sport of boxing. I have been to many fights. I recall going to Las Vegas with my business partner Sam Evans and my friend Jack Tricket who was a boxing promoter and manager in Manchester for many years. We went to watch the Tyson versus Bruno fight.

Jack managed to get us into the weigh-in for the big fight and there I met my hero, Muhammed Ali, and Sugar Ray Leonard. I also met Willie Pastrano, the former World Light Heavyweight champion, who years before had fought my friend from Cardiff, Joe Erskine. Joe beat Willie and I asked him about the fight, he told me Joe was the best boxer he ever fought. Jack also liked rugby league and came on a few trips to France with Kel Coslett and myself to watch Great Britain versus France games. I also bumped into Bill Mordey, who was the rugby league correspondent when I was at North Sydney. He was the manager of Jeff Fenech, the then World Featherweight Champion. I met Jeff and he told me he loved his rugby league. It was a great day and I met many of my heroes." However, Jim never got involved in boxing as a participant: "I did box a little at school, but I was too big so I could not get many to fight me; that was about it."

Jim progressed on to join Cardiff RFC, which was the leading rugby union club in Wales: "In my final years at school I was involved in summer sports such as athletics and I was a shot putter, but the main sport for me was rugby union. When I joined Cardiff I was in the youth team. As I developed I did get opportunities in the Cardiff Athletic side (the 'Rags' – the second team) and then the first team.

I owed a lot to the coaches down in Wales. Fred Croster and Sid

Judd nurtured me at school in the skills necessary to make the grade along with the coaches at the Arms Park. One player who helped me a great deal was the former Cardiff second-rower John Price. He showed me all the tricks of the trade and then some. He always seemed to have time to talk and point out things I could do to better my game. He is still a great friend to this day. Another younger player also used to talk with me about the game. He was Ian Robinson, and we formed the Cardiff second-row against the Barbarians just before I came north. He was later capped by Wales."

Sid Judd's faith in Jim clearly paid dividends as the young player started to establish himself. And his talent was noticed by others as he progressed through the ranks to be chosen for the Welsh Youth team.

Jim played four times for the Welsh Youth XV in March and April 1963. On 14 March, he played in a 0–0 draw with the Welsh Secondary Schools side. It was a floodlit match at Newport's Rodney Parade ground, played in "mud and lashing rain" according to the *Western Mail*. The report also noted that "Jim Mills (Cardiff) nearly 18-stone, proved a battering ram in the second-row."

Jim recalls: "I had made my debut in the Cardiff first XV at 18 years old in September 1963. Before then I was in the Welsh Youth squad and on 2 March 1963 I was selected for the Welsh Youth trial at Aberavon in the second row, I had a bit of confidence as I had been involved in the Welsh Youth squad since the 1961–62 season. Our opponents had been selected from the Welsh Youth squad also and on the left wing for the Whites was Frank Wilson.

Saturday 13 April 1963 was one of my proudest days in rugby. I captained the Welsh Youth XV against the Combined Midland Colts XV at the Moseley FC's The Reddings ground against a strong side made up from the various Colts teams from the top rugby union clubs in the Midlands.

Stuart Ferguson played on the left wing and my second row partner was M. J. Leighton of Pontypool. We won 16–0 and I was pleased with my own game especially with being the captain."

Against the Combined Midlands XV, the *Western Mail* said that the Welsh Youth side were superior throughout the match, and that "Mills, the Welsh captain, and wing forward Moyle were the pick of a good visiting pack..."

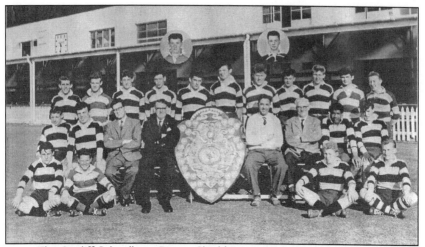

The Cardiff Schoolboys Dewar Shield team. Back: Thomas, I. Patterson Jones, Harris, B. Eliot, Jim, F. Phillips, not known; middle: R. Hill, B. Foster, not known, D. Brown, B. Bulpin; front: D. Irvins, not known, B. Collins, Pilchard Ron Hill and Dennis Brown later joined Castleford and Widnes respectively.

Wales Youth squad 1962–63 at Cardiff Arms Park.

7

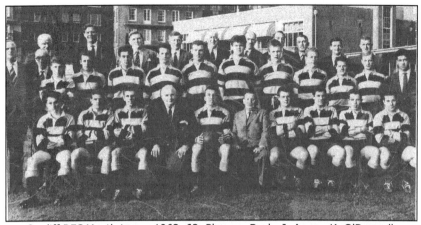

Cardiff RFC Youth team, 1962–63. Players: Back: J. Avery, K. O'Donnell, M. Thomas, P. Thomas, B. Ryan, J. Mills, I. Robinson, R. Ferry, D. Irving, P. Brennan; front: Not known, J .Carey, G. Thomas, Hubert Johnson, C. Prescott, Les Jones, G. Jones, C. Jones, I. Mathews, R. Pragnell. Committee: D. Brown. D. Davies. J. Spillane. P. Goodfellow. S. Bowes, W. Wilkins. A. T. Thomas. G. Porter, not known, G. Davies, B. Mark, B. Lewis, F. Trott

Welsh Youth XV	
M. K. HOWE, Bridgend	15
S. F. FERGUSON, Swansea	11
A. L. DENNIS, Neath	12
B. PRICE, Neath	13
I. J. JONES, Pontardulais	14
D. I. IVINS, Cardiff	10
G. G. THOMAS, Llanelly	9
J. V. JONES, Cardiff	1
V. C. PERRINS, Newport	2
P. E. MORGAN, Resolven	3
J. MILLS (Capt.), Cardiff	4
M. J. LEIGHTON, Pontypool	5
E. BOWEN, Pontardulais	6
E. J. CAMPODONIC, Pembroke	8
P. M. M. MOYLE, New Tredegar	7

1963 Welsh Youth XV that beat the Combined Midlands XV 16–0. Jim captained the side.

THE WELSH YOUTH XV.
(RED)

15 ‡R. HOPE	... ...	Pontypridd
11 S. FERGUSON	... ...	Swansea
12 I. MATHEWS		Cardiff
13 M. BISHOP	... ...	Pontardulais
14 I. J. JONES	... ...	Pontardulais
10 ‡E. A. C. MOGFORD	... ...	Newport
9 ‡D. R. H. HARRIES (Capt.)		Carmarthen Athletic
1 ‡A. C. WILLIAMS	... ...	New Tredegar
2 V. C. PERRINS	... ...	Newport
3 §E. MORGAN ...	... ...	Resolven
4 ‡J. MILLS	...	Cardiff
5 G. ROBERTS ...		Felinfoel
6 P. M. MOYLE	... ...	New Tredegar
7 E. BOWEN	... ...	Pontardulais
8 P. M. W. WATTS	... ...	Girlings

Left: The Welsh Youth XV that played England Schools at Twickenham in 1963.

Below: The line-ups in the match programme for Cardiff versus the Barbarians – the match celebrated the opening of Cardiff's floodlights.

	Cardiff					Barbarians	
1.	A. DREW		FULL BACKS		15.	S. WILSON	Oxford University and Scotland
2.	F. WILSON	Right Wing	THREE-QUARTERS	Left Wing	14.	C. P. SIMPSON	R.M.A. Sandhurst
3.	H. M. ROBERTS ★ (CAPTAIN)	Right Centre		Left Centre	13.	M. K. FLYNN	Wanderers and Ireland
4.	M. RICHARDS	Left Centre		Right Centre	12.	M. S. PHILLIPS	Fylde and England
5.	R. A. WILLS	Left Wing		Right Wing	11.	S. J. WATKINS	Newport and Wales
6.	T. J. McCARTHY	Stand-off	HALF BACKS	Stand-off	10.	D. H. CHISHOLM	Melrose and Scotland
7.	W. HULLIN	Scrum-half		Scrum-Half	9.	A. J. HASTIE	Melrose and Scotland
8.	C. H. NORRIS ★	Prop	FORWARDS	Prop	1.	R. J. McLOUGHLIN	Gosforth and Ireland
9.	W. J. THOMAS ★	Hooker		Hooker	2.	A. R. DAWSON	Wanderers and Ireland
10.	A. R. PENDER	Prop		Prop	3.	N. SUDDON	Hawick
11.	I. ROBINSON	Second Row		2nd Row	4.	A. M. DAVIS	Royal Navy and England
12.	J. MILLS	Second Row	Referee: Mr. D. G. WALTERS (Gowerton)	2nd Row	5.	B. E. V. PRICE	Newport and Wales
13.	E. R. WILLIAMS	Blind-side		Blind-side	6.	J. P. FISHER	R.H.S.F.P. and Scotland
14.	C. HOWE	No. 8	KICK-OFF 7.30 p.m.	No. 8	7.	J. W. TELFER	Melrose and Scotland
15.	D. J. HAYWARD ★	Open-side		Open-side	8.	D. P. ROGERS	Bedford and England

★ Internationals

9

Two days later, on 15 April, the Welsh Youth XV played the English Schools XV. The Welsh Secondary Schools XV had beaten the English Schools XV 14–6 earlier in the month at Cardiff Arms Park. The players selected had to be aged under–19 on 1 January 1963. The English players mainly came from grammar schools, the leading public schools, such as Rugby School, were not represented.

The English Schools XV won narrowly, 16–14. *The Times's* rugby correspondent commented that the teams were "two accomplished sides who played brilliant rugby in an exciting match." The Welsh team scored two tries to one from the English side, although the Welsh pack dominated their opponents for much of the game. Wales were ahead by one point going into the game's closing minutes, but a penalty after a "fierce struggle" on the Welsh line saw the English side narrowly win.

The *Western Mail* correspondent also enjoyed the encounter: "One of the most depressing rugby seasons for years ended on a note of high optimism yesterday when two skilful, speedy teams almost burst their young hearts with enthusiastic endeavour in the 19-age group youth international at Twickenham. That they were pipped by a penalty kick by English full-back RW Newton in the dying minutes was no disgrace to the Welsh Youth XV."

The Welsh captain that afternoon was scrum-half David Harries. Jim's second-row partner was Gerald Roberts of Felinfoel. Stuart Ferguson, another player who later went north, was retained on the left wing for this game. Only seven players involved at Twickenham for the Welsh Youth had played against Midland Colts. For the English Schools XV, Keith Slater was on the left wing, who starred for Wakefield Trinity in the early 1970s. The Welsh Youth XV was:

R. Hope, S. Ferguson, I. Matthews (Cardiff), M. Bishop, I.J. Jones, E.A. Mogford, D.R. Harris, A.C. Williams, V.C. Perrins, E. Morgan, J. Mills (Cardiff), G. Roberts, P.M. Moyle, P.M.W. Watts, E. Bowen.

A week later, the Welsh Youth side played a French Juniors XV at Cardiff Arms Park, and lost 9–0. John Billot, writing in the *Western Mail*, was shocked by the violent play: "French rugby has taught us the value of forwards being able to run, swerve and handle the ball adroitly. But at the Arms Park on Saturday they supplied us with a lesson that was a direct throwback to the days when rugby was a free-for-all and the Roman legionaries used a Briton's, or anyone else's, head that happened to be handy as a ball.

This was, without exaggeration, the roughest, toughest forward combat I have seen for some considerable time. The hot blood of the Basques never dropped below simmering temperature and some of the misdeeds of the French forwards made this a match to be held as an example of how national fervour can debase the game.

I blame the French players for the battle that developed. Wales, admittedly, were by no means innocent parties once it was realised that it was going to be that kind of game; but essentially it was a case of fight back with very little barred on take a hammering.

Wales chose to retaliate, and who could blame them? The powerful French front row charged into the scrums where a lot of old fashioned nonsense occurred... referee Arthur Luff (England) ...cannot have controlled a more difficult match." Billot did note that "Mills and Gerald Roberts (Felinfoel) generally jumped and won the lineout and rucked with rare vigour and zeal."

He concluded: "France thoroughly deserved their victory – their ninth in a row over the Welsh Youth. But in their team they appear to have some of the most dangerous men France has produced since Robespierre and we don't want to the 'The Terror' in a new form stalking our rugby fields."

In the WRU's booklet *50 years of Welsh Youth Rugby 1949–1999* (which, not surprisingly mentions many players who subsequently played rugby league) is an article by Ieuan Evans, who was appointed coach of the Welsh YRU team for the 1962–63 season, a position he held for 17 years. He includes a long list of "talented players". Jim Mills is the seventh name in the list, although as he is near others from the 1962–63 season, the list is probably in chronological order.

Jim made 16 first team appearances for Cardiff in the 1963–64 and 1964–65 seasons. He was awarded a cap in 1963–64 by Cardiff Athletic – Cardiff RFC's second team, known as the 'Rags' – in recognition of the number of appearances he had made for them.

Jim made his first team debut for Cardiff on 14 September 1963, at Cardiff Arms Park, against London Welsh. He played in the second row, and Cardiff lost 14–11. A Cardiff defensive error near the end presented the winning try to London Welsh. Cardiff were looking for their first win of the season after a poor start.

At that time, Cardiff played all their home matches in the stadium that also hosted the Welsh national team. The site where the club currently play was used by the Glamorgan cricket team for their matches. In 1967, the cricketers moved to their current ground, Sophia Gardens, and in 1970, the club moved to their present home, leaving the main stadium for the national team. It was subsequently redeveloped into the magnificent Millennium Stadium of today.

Jim returned to the second team, and next played for the senior team three times in three days over the Christmas period. On Boxing Day, he played in a 24–3 victory at the Arms Park against Welsh Academicals, and scored his first try for the senior side. JBG Thomas commented in his report in the *Western Mail* that "Mills and O'Shea were active in the tight and loose" and "J. Mills, a promising young second-row man, charged over from a line-out for an unconverted try."

The next day, Cardiff beat Watsonians 31–6. The Scottish club were on tour in South Wales, and playing their third match in three days. John Billot said in the *Western Mail* that "[Watsonians] skipper Derek Kidd and his lighter pack never gave up in a rousing tussle with the hard rucking Rowlands, Mills, Norris and the other Cardiff men." The next day, Cardiff then travelled to Kingsholm to beat Gloucester 14–3.

Another three month spell in the second team followed, before Jim was selected for one of the season's major matches, a visit to Swansea on 31 March, just after the Easter weekend. Cardiff won 13–0. It was Cardiff's third match in three days. They extended their unbeaten run to 18 matches, and it was their second victory at St Helens in six seasons. The *Western Mail* report said that "[Cliff] Howe gave inspiring aid to Keith Rowlands, Jim Mills, John O'Shea and Elved Morgan in the always lively forward combat."

Jim played his final match of the season on 23 April, a 10–3 win at Pontypool. It was Cardiff's penultimate match of the season, and his appearances in the first team had all been good experience for a 19-year-old.

In September 1964, Jim was selected for Cardiff's third match of the season, a midweek encounter with Bristol. He had started the season in the second team. Cardiff won comfortably, 23–3. The match was watched by the Fijian rugby team, who had just arrived to start their British tour. Dressed in traditional grey skirts and dark blazers, they were welcomed by the crowd. He kept his place against London Welsh, when Cardiff scored 48 points, and had notched 139 in their first four matches. In a 35–3 win at Penarth, the *Western Mail* noted that "At forward Howe and Pender were the best, with Thomas, Williams and Mills working hard under the leadership of Norris". Penarth's points were the first try that Cardiff had conceded that season.

Jim kept his place for the visit of Coventry to the Arms Park on 19 September, who were then one of England's stronger clubs. The home side won comfortably, 19–9, scoring five tries with two conversions. Four days later, on Wednesday 23 September, Gloucester came to the Arms Park for another England versus Wales encounter. After this match, Cardiff had won their first six matches against club opposition, and scored 157 points, conceding just 30. But their West Country opponents ran them close before going down 16–9. However, once again Cardiff did not concede a try.

Before the return match against Penarth, John Billot commented in the *Western Mail:* "Ian Robinson... makes his first team debut for Cardiff on Wednesday against Penarth at the Arms Park... He joins Jim Mills, who has been playing excellently since his first-team promotion against Bristol. Mills has played in the past five games alongside W.G. Davies, who is dropped for the first time this season." The match report said: "Jim Mills was outstanding as Cardiff's best forward, jumping to control the lineout, charging through, rucking forcefully and making his mark in other directions when needed." Cardiff won 14–0.

Cardiff's unbeaten run ended on 3 October, when Newport, captained by David Watkins, came to the Arms Park and won 10–5. The *Western Mail* said that they played badly and squandered chances. Jim, however, was again praised in the paper: "The packs of forwards battled away hard; rarely conceding anything and for Cardiff Thomas, Mills and Hayward were consistently good."

The biggest match Jim played for Cardiff was against the Barbarians on Wednesday 7 October 1964, the inaugural match for the Arms Park floodlights. While floodlighting was well established in association football, both rugby codes had shown little interest in the use of artificial lights. A 15,000 crowd came on a wet evening to watch a Barbarians side that included 13 full international, including the Melrose and Scotland half-back partnership of D.H. Chisholm and A.J. Hastie, R.J. McLoughlin of Gosforth and Ireland, B.E.V. Price of Newport and Wales, Jim Telfer, the great Melrose and Scotland flanker and 'Budge' Rogers of Bedford and England

The Barbarians won 12–8. *The Times* commented that "It was the

80th game between the clubs, but the first under floodlighting. The score did not greatly matter. What mattered most was the question whether or not floodlit rugby football, as inaugurated in this match, would be to the liking of the Cardiff enthusiasts, and the answer, undoubtedly, was yes."

In the *Western Mail*, J.B.G. Thomas wrote that: "Obviously the Cardiff selectors must now study their side closely and attempt to revitalise it. I would not condemn the young players, Robinson and Mills, who possess the right qualities, but sadly lack experience which is not of their fault, but I feel there is need to bring back older men."

The match programme included pen pictures of the Cardiff players. Jim's was precise. It gave his occupation as a 'driver' and said: "Is newcomer to the 1st XV this season, having graduated through Youth and Athletic sides. Lively and hard-working, is a strong young player."

The following Saturday, Jim scored his only try of the 1964–65 season for Cardiff in an 8–6 win at Northampton. The *Western Mail* reported: "Five minutes after the interval the victory of which Cardiff had always looked capable, began to take shape. Jim Mills, quite one of the best forwards, burst through from a lineout to score a try which Alan Drew converted."

Jim played his last match for Cardiff in a 3–0 win at Aberavon on 12 October. He contacted the Cardiff secretary to withdraw from the next match, away to Cambridge University. On Friday 16 October, the *Western Mail* carried a short report by JBG Thomas: "Yesterday the Halifax RL club announced that they had signed Cardiff's 20-year-old, 17 stone second row forward Jim Mills. The signing-on fee is not disclosed but it is understood to be more than £2,000. Mills informed the Cardiff club yesterday of his decision and was introduced to the Halifax club by their Cardiff-born centre C. Dixon, who played with Mills for the Cardiff youth side a few years ago.

Mills had been showing good form for Cardiff, a side which has been watched by rugby league scouts since the start of the season. Both M. Richards and F. Wilson, Cardiff's young threequarters, have been approached as well as several other young Welsh club players."

Jim had first been approached before the match against Coventry on 19 September: "I was walking up Westgate Street towards the gates at the Arms Park to get ready for the Coventry game when a voice called out to me: 'Excuse me Jim, could I have a word with you please?' I found out later the gentleman calling to me was Eddie Davies from Pontypool, who was a scout for the Halifax Rugby League club. He asked me if I would be interested in talking to the northern club with a view to signing with them. If I wasn't interested then that was that and no hard feelings. I was taken by surprise, but as I was unemployed at the time that influenced my response. I said that if the money was right I was obviously interested. That was enough for Eddie who knew the score about chatting up Welsh players to 'go north' when stood outside the main gates of the Arms Park and he vanished from sight.

My answer was enough for Halifax who pursued me relentlessly until I eventually agreed to speak with them. Actually it was my old mate, Colin Dixon, who recommended me to the Thrum Hall club as he was playing for Halifax at the time. It was a fellow Welshman who was the club secretary, Bill Hughes, who got things cracking. So from the date of the Coventry game, 19 September 1964, things moved on a pace and I went up to Halifax to meet the board of directors, agreed a signing on fee, £4,000, discussed my living arrangements in the town sorted out everything needed should I sign and travelled back down to Wales to have a final think about the move. The money would come in handy and in 1964 it was quite a tidy sum considering my financial situation. There was now no rush and push to sign, things were agreed and it was just down to me to say when."

After the Aberavon match, Jim rang the Cardiff club secretary and said, "I will be unavailable for the game against Cambridge University and any further games for Cardiff as I have signed as a professional player for Halifax". He recalls that a couple of the Cardiff committee members tried to talk him out of leaving, but it was too late, he had already signed the forms and was on his way to a whole new ball game.

Jim always played in the second row in rugby union. He believes that his strengths as a rugby union player were "my pace, and I was always physically strong. At the line-outs I could jump, and generally I was fit and athletic." Jim remembers playing with the Williams brothers, Lloyd, Elwyn and Tony, who were brothers of the great Bleddyn. Howard Norris, John Price, Cliff Howe, John Hickey, Billy Thomas, Ian Robinson, Billy Hullin, Alun Priday, John O`Shea, Frank Wilson, Tommy and Dennis McCarthy and Graham Davies were all regular team-mates.

15

Dai Hayward was another Cardiff star, at wing-forward, and Keith Rowlands played twice for Wales in the 1964–65 season. Jim recalls: "Most of the first team were Welsh internationals and some had played for the British Lions." Maurice Richards was making his way in the first team when Jim left and later followed Jim north to play for Salford.

Before he won a regular first-team place, Jim played in the second and youth teams. From the youth team he particularly recalls Bob Ryan, Gareth Jones, Chris Jones, Colin Prescott, Kevin O`Donnell, Islwyn Mathews and Peter Thomas, who is now the current owner and chairman of Cardiff Blues, who with his brother Stan, became very successful businessmen.

Jim never received any payment for playing for Cardiff. He recalls: "Players from the valleys got their fares, we had a meal on training nights and match days, and there were free drinks. There was talk about players being paid at other clubs, but never at Cardiff. The club was the premier one in Wales, and attracted the top players. If a player made his name in the Valleys, they would join Cardiff. After I left, Barry John and Gareth Edwards were the stars. Most of the players were salesmen or school teachers. Not many did physical working class jobs."

Formal coaching in rugby union at this time was very limited. Jim recalls: "On training nights, we would sign in, and the team captain would take us out onto the pitch. We would do a few laps and some sprints. They had a few weights for us to use under the stand. We would practice scrummaging, and have a talk at the end of the session. It wasn't very professional, just fitness training mainly. We did two or three evenings a week." And, given his career in rugby league, it is worth noting that Jim was never sent off when playing rugby union.

Jim, many years later, reckoned that the signing for Halifax when 20 years old was possibly one of the two major mistakes he made in his career. Not that it was a mistake to sign for Halifax but it was in the timing of his signing. He commented: "I always regretted going north so early. Cardiff were sorry that I left. I was playing regularly in the first team. If I'd stayed I could have played for Wales. It was silly to go north when I was so young. It was an immature decision."

Jim is remembered in Wales, especially by the coaches who worked with the Cardiff Youth and Welsh Youth squads. The official responsible for selecting and coaching these sides at Cardiff was Henry Hurley, who was involved with them for 25 years. He was interviewed in a special issue of *Welsh Rugby* magazine around 1976. When asked who was the most outstanding back and forward to represent Cardiff Youth, Mr Hurley chose Terry Holmes as the back, and chose Jim Mills as the outstanding forward. The article by Graham Evans says that "Jim's power, pace and knowledge would have held him in great stead had he remained with the Union game." The article also says that Jim was "an outstanding Youth player".

In November 2012 Jim spoke at the Cardiff RFC Former Players Association dinner. Graham Davies, the association's secretary, wrote to thank him and said that "Everyone thought that your speech was wonderful and that you were the best guest speaker we have had... As I looked at the people at the dinner I realised that most would never have seen you play (or know that you had played) the Union game – they would know about you solely through your glittering League career. I wonder if you ever think about what would have happened if you had not gone north? I'm sure that you would have been up there with the "greats" of the union game."

David Watkins went north after Jim, joining Salford in 1967. He recalls: "I first saw Jim when he was playing for Cardiff Youth. He was a tall, slim second-rower and everyone said, 'Watch this kid, he will be a good 'un.' Another of Jim's mates was the late Colin Dixon, who was a scrum-half at Cardiff Youth. Jim was obviously a talented player and I know that he was extremely well thought of in the Cardiff club. The difference between Jim and the other second-rowers was that Jim was not just a pusher in the scrum and a jumper in the line-out, he was quick with the pace of a middle back. Unlike the two second-rowers that I was brought up with, Brian Price and Bill Morris, both cracking rugby union forwards, Jim had that extra bit of class using his speed. He was strong in the pack pushing and with him being such a big, strong lad he was excellent in the line-outs."

Would Jim have played for Wales, and even the British Lions? In both codes of rugby, forwards do not fully mature until their mid–20s. At the age of 20 Jim had won a regular place in the Cardiff first team, and was regularly playing against the top players at club level, and some of the leading internationals. He was getting favourable coverage in the media. Gary Protheroe, who was one of the forwards that Henry Hurley felt Jim had surpassed as a young player, went to win international honours. Had he continued to develop as he had in his time at Cardiff, he certainly would have reached full international level. But in 1964 once a player had signed for a rugby league club, his career in rugby union was finished.

Jim would face new challenges in Halifax.

At work on the farm around 1960.

Keeping the cattle under control.

David on holiday with Mum and Dad in Porthcawl, on the beach.

Soon after signing for Halifax in 1964. Back row (from left): Jim, Charlie Renilson, Colin Dixon, Stan Fearnley, Terry Ramshaw, David Jones; front: Ron James, Peter Goodchild, Barry Robinson.

Three Cardiff rugby league veterans: Johnny Freeman and Billy Boston with Jim. Johnny and Billy went to school together and played at the CIAC club, along with Joe Erskine, the famous boxer. Jim played with Johnny at Halifax.

2. Gone north: Halifax 1964 to 1968

Jim was joining a club that was one of the oldest in rugby league, having first played in 1873. They had been a strong club before the split in rugby football in 1895, and became one of the Northern Union's foundation clubs in 1895.

The club had been one of the game's leading sides in the first half of the 1950s, but had the misfortune to often face a powerful Warrington side in finals. They were runners up in the League Championship three times in this period, and were twice losing Challenge Cup Finalists. One of those was in one of the sport's great occasions, the 1954 Odsal replay, when around 120,000 people saw them lose 8–4 to Warrington. The Yorkshire Cup was won in 1954–55 and 1955–56, but there were no more final appearances for the rest of the 1950s. The team declined and in 1959–60 finished 22nd in the league.

The appointment of Albert Fearnley as first team coach in 1961 started a revival. Andrew Hardcastle, the club historian, comments in *The Thrum Hall Story* that by 1963, "[The] Halifax team was a good one again. Albert Fearnley... had developed a pack with an excellent blend – the toughness of Ken Roberts and John Shaw; the size and strength of Jack Scroby and ... prop Frank Fox; the skills of Terry Fogerty and the running and tackling of Charlie Renilson and former centre Colin Dixon, whose move into the forwards saw him develop as an all-time-great."

When Jim joined the club, they played at Thrum Hall, their traditional home with a slope and great atmosphere for big matches. But later, in 1998, they moved to The Shay, to share with the local football club. Thrum Hall was sold, most of the limited proceeds eventually being used to pay off debts.

Rugby league was in a transition period when Jim moved to the game. The sport had just returned to one division, having cut short a move to two divisions, which only last for two seasons. The great crowds of the post-war boom had gone, and some clubs were facing severe competition from football, particularly some in West Yorkshire, where Leeds United had become one of football's leading clubs. The game had been slow to adopt floodlights, and had almost no base outside its traditional areas. But clubs were still a major part of their communities, there were great players at the top of the game, and the sport's big occasions still attracted good crowds. The game's authorities were also starting to consider changes to its rules, to make it more attractive to watch.

Halifax today is a town of about 82,000 people, and today the main centre of Calderdale Borough Council. Apart from the building society which bore its name, traditionally weaving mills and engineering were an important part of the town's economy, along with manufacturing confectionary. As well as the rugby league team, Halifax Town FC had a long tradition in the lower reaches of the Football League, although in recent years they have dropped out of the league, reformed as AFC Halifax and are now playing in Conference North.

Jim had arranged to travel up to Yorkshire and sign for Halifax on Wednesday 14 October, but when he stepped off the train there was no one to meet him. He made his way to Thrum Hall and when club secretary Bill Hughes saw Jim he was amazed, but realised that he had made a mistake with the day Jim was due to arrive. Hughes took Jim around to see Mrs Greenwood, a widow who provided digs for him and looked after him well. The house was just off Gibbet Street only two minutes away from the Thrum Hall ground.

So with a little trepidation Jim embarked, aged 20, on a journey into a new game, in a new place in the north of England. He recalls: "I had watched rugby league on the BBC *Grandstand* programme with Eddie Waring commentating. I had never been to a live game, but usually watched the Challenge Cup Final on television. It seemed glamorous. I remember watching Billy Boston bumping people out of the way. Billy was from Cardiff; and at Halifax so were Johnny Freeman and Colin Dixon. I had never been to the north of England. Moseley in the west midlands was the furthest north I had been.

Albert Fearnley was the first team coach, and Ken Dean and Stan Kielty ran the 'A' team. I felt that Albert didn't ask for me, Colin Dixon had recommended me to the directors but Albert already had a good pack. At training I was asked to sprint against Charlie Renilson and beat him. Then I was asked to catch balls. But I never felt he was keen on me, I was not his choice. But Ken Dean and Stan Kielty both gave me great advice and support. They had both been half-backs in the great Halifax side of the 1950s.

I learnt to 'play the ball', but rugby league for a forward was a

22

completely different game from union. It was continuous, with no breaks. I found the pace was fast, and the tackling tougher. In Welsh rugby union, the players said that rugby league was tougher and faster than union. I never met anyone who did not say the same.

The scrums were not that different; I was in the second row and gave a push. The front row was the key place. There weren't as many forwards as in union. Of course they were competitive scrums, not like now, where the side feeding the scrum get the ball. In union I was good at line-outs, there was no lifting then, we had to jump for the ball and I was good at that. But there weren't line-outs in rugby league.

I found I got the ball more in rugby league. In union there were loose mauls, but in rugby league I had to learn when to pass and how to find a gap. I had to improve my passing, and not to hold the ball above my head as I did in union. It took me a while to grasp the game. Some players slot in easier than others. I became fitter as I played league, and lost half a stone. The tackling was tougher, different from rugby union. I had to learn how to protect myself.

The players were very friendly, especially Colin Dixon, Johnny Freeman and Ronnie James. James was from Maesteg, played at full-back and was a great goalkicker. Another good friend who took me under his wing was Hughie Duffy, who was coming to the end of his career with Halifax. He had previously played for Salford, and was a Scottish rugby union international. I had many a meal with him and his wife Irene, and they are still my great friends to this day. Another good team-mate was Ian Foye, an Australian hooker from Bundaberg.

But I was very homesick. I was put in digs with Mrs Greenwood. My room had a skylight, but no window. I would lie on my bed and wonder what I had done by coming north. It was OK when I was out with the players, but it was not my home environment. I missed my mother's cooking, and had never been away from home before. I thought about going home, but Colin said to stick at it. Later, I moved into another lodging when Mrs Greenwood became ill. I moved into a public house, the Allen Fold in the King Cross area in Halifax with Cynthia and Frank Budge and I was well looked after.

We got good crowds and I enjoyed playing at Thrum Hall. It took me time to settle in, and I did not get much help from Albert Fearnley, unlike Vince Karalius at Widnes who did develop me.

I used to go around with Colin Dixon. One evening we went to see a

23

film, and then went ten-pin bowling. There was a bar there, but we didn't have a drink – I didn't go out drinking the night before a game. But someone had seen us there, told the club and we were dropped.

Two of the first people I got to know were Les Pearce, who later became the Wales Rugby League coach and had played union for Swansea, and John Thorley, a former Welsh rugby league international, who also played for Great Britain when we won the World Cup in France in 1954, and had played union for Neath. They became big friends of mine. I still speak to Les regularly. Former Welsh union international full-back Garfield Owen had left Halifax by then and was with Keighley, but he still worked in the town, and sold me my first car, a Ford Zephyr."

Albert Fearnley was a folk hero to the Halifax fans. A former hard as nails, a big bustling back-row forward he had attained county level as a player and was unfortunate to be in an era when almost every team had at least one cracking back rower. Fearnley made 207 appearances for Halifax from 1950 to 1956, and was one of the key players in that successful era for the club. He subsequently joined Featherstone, and finished his career as player-coach at Batley before returning to Halifax as first team coach in 1961.

Fearnley had let it be known that as the coach he wanted a couple of class backs. Suddenly the board of directors produced a 20 year old 'rookie' forward. In those days the directors decided which players would sign for the club and also often selected the team as well.

Jim made his Halifax debut for the 'A' team against Leeds at Headingley on 24 October 1964. But with an established pack, and other players like Barney Hardcastle and Bernard Scott available in the 'A' team in case of injuries or suspensions, Fearnley left Jim in the 'A' team for over a year. While he clearly had to learn this new game, it is surprising that he was not given opportunities as a substitute in the first team to gain more experience, especially against some of the weaker sides in the league. Halifax 'A' finished 6th of 16 clubs in their league, the Yorkshire Senior Competition; Jim scored two tries in 13 second-row appearances.

Halifax's first team won the Championship that season. The league had reformed into one division of 30 clubs for 1964–65. Halifax finished seventh in the table, but fought their way through to the final. At Swinton they faced a St Helens team who were strong favourites, but the Thrum Hall side won 15–7, to become Northern Rugby League Champions for the first time since 1907.

"Halifax had sorted me out with a job at Asquith's in heavy engineering, and the first day at work the foreman met me and said that he had been told that I was a driver" Jim recalls. "I replied that I was and he said 'Right, climb aboard that and we will see how you go.' I had the shock of my life when I looked at the vehicle he wanted me to drive, it was an overhead crane used for moving huge machines and engines that were made on the shop floor. I told him that I had never been inside one of them, let alone driven one. 'You'll be OK, just take it steady and you will pick it up soon' he replied. Now, on the shop floor were some former rugby league players who worked together as engineers. They all were Welsh and three were connected to Halifax and were great mickey-takers. Part of my job as a crane driver was to turn over the machines the lads were working on. They were all on bonuses and wanted things done quickly. They used to shout up at me, sat there above them and learning the job. Stan Sparks, Les Pearce and John Thorley were the Halifax men and Mel Meek was the Fartowner. Many a bolt was thrown at my crane to gee me up."

Jim had to wait until he was 21 years old to make his first team debut, against Warrington at Thrum Hall on 20 November 1965. He had twice before been a non-playing substitute, against Doncaster at Thrum Hall and Hull K.R. at Craven Park in October. Club historian and life-long supporter Andrew Hardcastle outlines that "Jim was young, raw, and took time to adapt to rugby league, but what a player he turned out to be. Unfortunately for Halifax, it was after he had moved on to other clubs, notably Widnes, but the Thrum Hallers deserve credit for bringing him into the game."

The rugby league historian, Robert Gate, a Halifax supporter, wrote in *Gone North* that "Halifax and the player himself must have wondered if they had made a mistake as injuries contrived to prevent the costly signing from breaking into the first team for over a year."

Jim recalls: "I was determined to play well and make the selectors consider me to play the week after as I had waited for this chance for a long time. I weighed up the opposition and had made a couple of good runs as well as tackling as much as anyone else. Then I caught sight of a gap in the Warrington defence and hit the ball up from a pass from our dummy half Dave Harrison. I thought I'll just shift this old looking

25

guy in front of me and I'm clear, so I raced into the gap at the side of this bloke and he just shifted his feet and caught me with his shoulder in my ribs. I was in shock. I shuddered like one of those cartoon characters in the old Walt Disney films who runs into a brick wall! As I was coming around one of our lads said, 'Are you OK Jim? You want to be careful about running into that bloke, he is one tough bugger, that's Charlie Winslade.' I thought, thanks for telling me now. Charlie was a Welshman from Maesteg; a rough, old fashioned forward who had seen off some of the hardest men in the game in his time."

Unfortunately for Jim, Halifax lost 7–2 to Warrington, their first defeat at Thrum Hall for over a year. He kept his place for an 8–4 win at Castleford, and a narrow 7–6 defeat at Thrum Hall to Leeds. He did not play on Christmas Day against Bradford Northern, but returned to the first team on New Year's Day in a 16–12 win at Featherstone. His only other first team was in a 15–11 victory over Bramley at Thrum Hall on 15 April, the team's third match in five days. All Jim's first team matches were in the second-row, though on three occasions towards the end of the season he played three times for the 'A' team as a prop. Altogether for the reserves he made 12 appearances in 1965–66, scoring two tries. A player Jim remembers well from this time is the Australian Lionel Williamson. The team was travelling over the Pennines on a wintery day, and the Queenslander insisted on stopping the coach so he could go and touch the snow, which he had never seen before.

In 1966–67 he was again in the 'A' team for much of the season, six times at prop and eight in the second row, scoring four tries. On 30 September Jim came off the bench for the first team in a 32–22 defeat at Castleford. He was then given a run in the first team in the second row over the Christmas and New Year period. He played in the second-row in a 30–7 loss away to Hull KR on 17 December, and played in three of the next four games, the final one being a 22–0 loss at Headingley on 27 January.

An opening was created for Jim when Ken Roberts, one of Halifax's regular props, left to join Bradford Northern at the end of February, in exchange for Stan Fearnley, a second-rower. Halifax gave Jim a chance at prop at Odsal on 4 March. Halifax won 23–13, with Fearnley scoring two tries. However, Jim kept his place for six of the next nine matches, and scored a couple of tries, against Batley and Featherstone, both at Thrum Hall. Halifax finished 11th, with 38 points from 34 matches.

The 1967–68 campaign started well for Jim. He had trained well in pre-season. The *Halifax Courier* commented before the annual pre-season charity match against Huddersfield at Fartown: "There is a surprise switch in the forwards. Towards the end of last season Jim Mills, normally a second-row man, was tried at open-side prop and seemed to be a success there. However, the directors have moved him to the blind side, and Jack Scroby, who was just as effective in the other prop position, will wear the number eight jersey."

However, Jim played in the second row for the first two games, a 20–8 defeat away to Hull KR and a 6–6 draw with Huddersfield at Thrum Hall. The back three forwards for Halifax were Jim, Terry Ramshaw and Stan Fearnley.

Jim moved to prop in a 24–16 win over Widnes, missed a defeat at Doncaster with a thigh injury, but then played the next seven games in the front row. He scored two tries in a match for the first time for Halifax's first team in a 27–18 win over Salford. Roland Tinker reported in the *Courier*: "...This was quickly followed by Mills's second. Big Jim is one who appreciates the ball distribution of [Jackie] Pycroft, for the tricky scrum-half gave it to him when Mills was in between two defenders. Another two closed in on him, but when Mills is moving near the line the defence might as well wave the white flag and surrender!" He added: "Mills was the game's best forward, not because he got those two tries, but because he had something constructive to offer, always looking round for support when he moved forward." Jim says that "I felt my game improved greatly when Jackie Pycroft signed for the club in 1966. He had a great pass, had me running into the gaps and would give me the ball at the perfect time. I thought he was a great player, who I felt was very much under-rated."

However, Jack Scroby came back into the team in the front row, and Jim returned to action in the second row, and only missed four matches before his final game for Halifax on Christmas Day.

On 13 October Jim experienced the first of his sendings off in rugby league. It was against Doncaster at Thrum Hall and his opponent was George Goodyear. Jim put up with messing about from George then snapped. George was dispatched for treatment and Jim to the dressing room by referee Eric Clay. He was banned for one match. On 4 November, he was sent off again, six minutes from the end of the match at York, and was given a two match ban.

Jim played against the 1967 Australians tourists on 29 November, and had clashed with the Australian forwards including Noel Kelly, who later became a good mate of Jim's. The Australians had a difficult tour, and although they won the test series 2–1 against Great Britain, lost nine out of 27 matches. However, they had one of their best matches against Halifax, and won 22–2.

Jim had got married in 1966, but there were problems, and they affected his rugby. Also, Halifax had signed some new players, including forwards Bill Kirkbride for £6,000 from Workington and Ian Crawshaw from Bradford. He felt unsettled, and even considered moving back to South Wales. Jim recalls: "My marriage was breaking up and I thought about retiring and returning to Cardiff. David Watkins rang me and asked me to go to Salford."

The move suited Halifax, who received a £4,000 fee from the Lancashire club, so made a profit on Jim's time at the club, and Salford wanted to reinforce what Jim recalls as "an aging pack". He signed for Salford in February. Up to Christmas Day, he had played in 21 of Halifax's first team matches, and had scored four tries. His last appearance for them was in an 18–2 defeat against Bradford Northern at Thrum Hall. A recurrence of a shoulder injury prevented Jim playing anymore for Halifax before he went to Salford. He had played 76 times for Halifax in just over four years, but half had been in the 'A' team.

Robert Gate concludes in *Gone North* about Jim's time at Thrum Hall: "As a young league player at Thrum Hall he was very raw but he was big and willing and responded to the fans' exhortations to 'go on Jim lad'. At that stage of his career Mills was about as subtle as a sledge-hammer but his battering-ram style endeared him to the Thrum Hall faithful. Even so, one thing that was not in short supply at Halifax at that time was good forwards and Mills could never be sure of first team football."

But Andrew Hardcastle was not the only one who was sorry to see him leave Thrum Hall: "I'd seen most of his games for the first team and second team," he remembers, "and watched him develop into a top rugby league player. Halifax had signed some great Welsh stars over the years, and Jim was the latest of them. The best was clearly still to come. Like those I stood alongside on the terraces, I would have preferred for him to have stayed."

3. A short stay at Salford

In joining Salford, Jim was moving to a club who had been a major force in the game in the 1930s, but had achieved little since. However, Brian Snape had become the club chairman, and was building a team that would become a major force in the late 1960s and early 1970s.

The club faced competition for support from Manchester United and Manchester City, and often played on Friday nights in this period. This was linked to developing a well-organised social club at the Willows.

One of the club's most significant signings was Welsh rugby union star David Watkins, who had come north from Newport in October 1967 for a record signing-on fee. Jim recalls that "David Watkins phoned me to sound me out about going to Salford. I knew David from our union days in South Wales, but we were not close friends. They had some good players in the backs, but the pack was getting on. I think they would have won more if they'd invested in the forwards."

Jim's short spell at the club was before they made some significant signings. England rugby union forward Mike Coulman came in October 1968, followed by two of Jim's former Cardiff team-mates, Colin Dixon from Halifax in December 1968 and Maurice Richards in 1969. In 1973, Keith Fielding was another high profile recruit. When Jim signed they were on the verge of a very successful period; had he settled at the club he could have been a part of that team.

Griff Jenkins was the Salford coach. Jim's new team-mates included Chris Hesketh, who was a British Lion in 1970 and 1974; Alan McInnes who was a fine back; Les Bettinson, who played at centre and won Cumberland County honours and scrum-half Jacky Brennan. The forwards included Peter Smethurst, Charlie Bott and Stuart Whitehead. Jim remembers "No matter how I tried my mind was still in a tangle with my problems at home. I just was not right in almost everything I did. I tried to concentrate on my rugby but being in such a poor mental state I found that I wanted to fight everyone instead of playing to the plan laid down by Griff. I thought the move to Salford would straighten me out with a change of team personnel and a Welsh coach, but I began to feel disinterested. It took me two hours to travel to training and home games. This was new to me because all my rugby, at the Arms Park and at Thrum Hall, had been near home. It was soon obvious that the move to Salford was not a good idea."

Jim made his Salford debut in the Challenge Cup against Blackpool at the Willows on 2 February 1968. The Red Devils won 16–5, and Jim kept his place for the next three matches, a defeat at Warrington, an 11–2 win at home to Leigh, and an 8–4 loss at Wakefield in the Challenge Cup. He recalls: "The final straw was when I was selected as substitute forward for the game after the Wakefield cup game against Warrington at home which we lost 14–6. Then I contracted a bad bout of flu and missed training on the Tuesday evening. I managed to get to training on the Thursday, but was dropped to the 'A' team for the next weekend's game. I received no explanation for being dropped from the first team and decided to stay away from the club because I was so fed up. I returned to Salford and trained again after a fortnight and asked for a meeting with Griff Jenkins. I told him that I wanted to get away from Salford and could not play at the moment. My career at Salford was short and sharp. I left in March intending to sort my life out in Halifax and definitely return home to Wales. Then, out of the blue, I got a phone call from Harry Womersley who had just become the chairman at Bradford Northern. He asked to meet me along with another board member, Jack Fricker, to talk about moving to Odsal.

I met them in a pub in Halifax and they said that I was still only 24 years old and pointed out that there was an Australian tour in 1970 with only a few top class props around. 'With a bit of luck you could make that tour Jim', Harry said, 'and coming to Odsal would cut out much of the travelling for training and home matches'. They gave me some sound advice and I realised that I had to pull myself together and get my sporting life back on track. My lifestyle had limited my finances and I needed to get back quickly earning from football. I changed my job too; leaving Asquith's to take a job as a drayman for Ramsden's brewery delivering beer to the pubs around Halifax."

Jim actually signed for Bradford Northern in July 1968, and started to establish himself at a new club, back in Yorkshire, and ironically with his former Halifax coach Albert Fearnley. Despite all his problems, Jim was not sent off while playing for Salford. Salford finished the season in ninth place in the league, with 22 wins from their 34 matches.

It is interesting to speculate how Jim's career might have developed had he settled at Salford. In 1969 the Red Devils reached the Challenge Cup Final, losing to Castleford at Wembley, and in the first five years of the 1970s won the Championship twice, the Lancashire Cup, the BBC2

Floodlit Trophy and were runners up in four other finals. But it was not until Jim joined Widnes, and was coached by Vince Karalius, that he fulfilled his potential in rugby league, and won more trophies than Salford managed in their spell as one of the sport's top teams.

Salford did try to sign Jim from Widnes a few years later on in his career. Jim recalls: "I was sorry I let Brian Snape down at Salford. He was a good man who I had great respect for, but I think he knew I had problems off the field. Little did I know that he would try to sign me again years later when I was at Widnes, so he must have forgiven me. Unfortunately for Salford, I would come back to haunt them in several finals and cup ties for Widnes, which we won."

Jim has always had a great interest in boxing.

Left: With Muhammad Ali in Las Vegas.

Right: Two heavyweights! With Henry Cooper before a Mike Tyson fight.

Bottom: Billy Boston, Jim, Ricky Hatton, Bob Blackwood and Sam Evans at a benefit dinner for Terry O'Connor at Widnes RLC.

4. A new start: Bradford Northern

Jim's move back across the Pennines took him to one of the sport's famous names. Bradford adopted the 'Northern' part of their name when the club split in 1907, with the other part of the club switching to association football and becoming Bradford Park Avenue FC. The name of the new club showed their identification with the Northern Union, the forerunner of the Rugby Football League.

In the post-war period they had been one of the sport's leading clubs, but from the mid–1950s a period of decline set in, and crowds dwindled in their giant bowl of a ground at Odsal. In December 1963 the club collapsed and withdrew from the League. However, a campaign in the city organised by Trevor Foster and Joe Phillips saw a new club, still with the Bradford Northern name, join the league. In their first season back, 1964–65, they finished 17th, but the next season they won the Yorkshire Cup, and climbed to seventh place. In the next two seasons they finished 5th and 6th respectively, so Jim was joining a club that was one of the stronger ones in the competition.

Today, Bradford has a population of just under 300,000; so the club had a much bigger potential supporter base than Halifax. However, it had competition at this time from two Football League teams, Bradford City and Bradford Park Avenue. Traditionally, Bradford's economy was based on textiles and wool, but this gradually declined after the Second World War, and today is more based on manufacturing and some tourism.

Coach Albert Fearnley had joined the club in 1966, and served it in various capacities for the next decade. So Jim would be reunited with his first rugby league coach, who had seemed to have little time for him at Halifax. However Jim recalls that "I checked with Harry Womersley before I signed that Albert Fearnley would support me, and Harry guaranteed that he would." Jim says that Womersley was "a true rugby league man, a great club chairman and managed the 1979 Great Britain tour of Australia and New Zealand. I owe him a great debt for keeping me in the game. Sadly, he died of Leukaemia some years back."

There was a strong Welsh influence at the club. Trevor Foster was there, who had 'gone north' from Newport in 1938. Jim has many memories of someone who was a major figure at the club, and had been one of the key people in the relaunch of Northern in 1964 after the club had collapsed at the end of 1963: "When we were training, we would see someone walking towards us in the dark, and it would be Trevor, who would come and support us. He was a great man to talk to about the game. I loved listening to him – he knew so much about the history of the game. When I came to Bradford I really got to know him. When I played for Wales, he would come into the dressing room, and offer to rub the players down. Later on he became president of the Welsh Past Players Association. I was the chairman, and used to offer him a lift. But he walked everywhere. 'Jimmy, the good Lord gave us these legs to walk, not sit in cars. He walked like a soldier. When I was chairman at Widnes, when Bradford came to play I would always invite him for a meal before the game. He loved the game so much, he was a great man. I was sorry to miss his funeral – I was on a cruise and couldn't get back."

In July 1967, Welsh rugby union international full-back Terry Price had been recruited from Llanelli for an £8,000 signing on fee. Another Welshman at the club was hooker Tony Fisher, who became a great friend of Jim's: "Tony joined the club from the RAF. He had been a boxing champion in the forces, and had played rugby union for Swansea. His brother Idwal also played for Swansea." They went on to play together for Wales and Great Britain.

Jim signed for the club on 19 July 1968, for a fee of £2,750. However, earlier in the year the club had been in financial trouble again, and out of the resulting turmoil, four players had been sold, but the club spent almost as much as the transfer fees they received in signing four new recruits.

However, Jim was seen as a good recruit for the club. Nigel Williams comments in his history of the club on this period, which saw the club drop down the table to finish 27th in 1970–71: "Of the players they bought, the majority, though good players in their own right, just did not seem to fit in at Northern. The exceptions being Neil Fox, who they bought on August 22nd 1969 for £5,500 from Wakefield Trinity, and Jim Mills..."

Jim recalls his arrival at Odsal: "I hadn't a clue what sort of welcome I would receive from Albert and hoped it would be more friendly than our first meeting. It was, because this time he knew I was joining his club and things were fine between us. When I arrived at

Odsal I felt it was like being at home in Wales. The dressing room seemed to be full of Welshmen. One was Terry Price, a Welsh rugby union international and a prolific kicker either out of hand or from a placed ball."

When Jim arrived at the club, the pack at Bradford included two forwards who played a large number of clubs: Terry Clawson and Geoff Clarkson. Jim recalls the latter as "a Wakefield lad who was a very good forward and played very well at Bradford." Albert's son, loose-forward Stan Fearnley, later played against Jim for Leeds against Widnes at Wembley. Cumbrian Frank Foster had been recruited from Hull KR. Jim says that he was "a very strong and hard man, who was respected throughout the game; a great forward." Other contenders for a place were Graham Joyce, Dave Hill, whose son Brendan later played at Odsal, Laurie Hinchliffe and two Australians, Noel Cavanagh and John McDonnell. They played for the club on short-term contracts in Jim's second season. They were later his team-mates at North Sydney. Jim remembers playing with Cavanagh in a game against Featherstone: "Noel was from Queensland. There was icy rain driving into us. Noel was like a frozen statue. 'It's warm today' I said to him. He was so cold he could hardly speak. He got in a hot bath after the game, he was in agony. Years late, David stayed at Noel's place in Bundaberg when he was on tour, and another time Noel's son stayed with us." Another member of the pack was Ken Roberts, a former colleague of Jim's at Halifax.

In the backs, Geoff Wrigglesworth, the former Leeds threequarter was a strong running international centre. One of the wingers was one of the game's fastest players, Berwyn Jones, a former international 100 metre record holder. Drew Broatch, who was Scottish and joined the club from Leeds, also played at centre or on the wing, as did another Welshman, Les Thomas, who later joined Keighley.

The half-backs included Dave Stockwell, a former Halifax stand-off who had joined the club in 1964; scrum-half Paul Daley, who had been one of Jim's team mates at Thrum Hall and Bak Diabira, who Jim says "went on to give great service to Bradford".

Two of the backroom staff were Fred Robinson, the kitman, and Ronnie Barrett, the masseur / physio. Jim says that "Fred was a great character, who was very good for team spirit. He was one of the longest serving kitmen in the game, and was still involved with the club when Super League started. Ronnie also gave long service to the club, and was the physio for the Great Britain side when we beat the Australians at Odsal in 1978."

One change from his previous clubs was that Jim was now clearly established as a front-rower, and played all his matches for Bradford at prop. Jim's debut for Bradford was against his former club, Salford. A try from Vaughan Thomas and goal from Terry Price were not enough to prevent Salford winning 11–5 at Odsal. Jim only missed four matches until 16 November, although two of his appearances were off the bench. His place in the front row was then taken by Peter Goddard, a young prop who had been signed from an amateur club in Oldham. Dave Hill and Terry Clawson were also contenders for a place in the front-row, although Clawson left a couple of months into the new season. Jim had been sent off against York at Odsal on 30 November, and was banned for two games. However, he had injured a knee in this game, which saw him miss a further nine matches.

Jim returned to first team action on 30 March, having missed 14 matches. Not having scored a try all season, he suddenly got three in four matches. He scored in an 18–7 win at Batley, got another in a 32–3 victory over Dewsbury at Odsal, and another in a 17–6 defeat at Huddersfield. Jim recalls: "I was considering asking Harry Womersley for an increase in pay with me scoring every week, but in the Huddersfield game I was sent off again for fighting. That finished me for the remainder of that season because I received a four match suspension." Goddard took his place at number eight again. Jim finished the season with 21 appearances including two off the bench.

Bradford finished the season in 19th place, with 16 wins and 18 defeats. In the Yorkshire Cup, Jim had played against Castleford in the semi-final, when Northern lost by one point at Odsal. In the Challenge Cup a comfortable win at Dewsbury was followed by defeat in a replay to Wakefield Trinity.

The 1969–70 season was only two weeks old when Northern signed Neil Fox from Wakefield Trinity for £5,500. Fox had won every honour in the game with Wakefield, where he had been for 13 years. Robert Gate in his biography of Fox comments that he was joining a club where the pack "was definitely big and tough. Not many teams took liberties with the likes of Jim Mills, Tony Fisher, Dave Hill, [Frank] Foster, Geoff Clarkson and Stan Fearnley." Jim recalls "Neil Fox was a

36

wonderful goalkicker and oozed class. When he joined the club, it gave everyone a lift. He was very powerful for a centre, did a great job for Bradford and was one of the best players I played with. I remember near the end of his career, when he returned to Bradford, he scored two tries against the Australians, and made it look so simple."

Jim started the team at number eight, and kept his place until 15 March, a 10–9 victory over Hull, when he left to join North Sydney. Laurie Hinchliffe took his place for the final six matches of the season. Northern climbed to 12th place in the table, but lost in the first rounds of the Yorkshire Cup and Challenge Cup, to Leeds and St Helens respectively. Jim again scored three tries, curiously twice against Hull KR, and then at home to Doncaster.

The Wales team had been revived in November 1968. Jim won a place in the first match of the 1969–70 season, against England at Headingley, and kept his place for the next three matches against England and France. On 5 March he was named in the British Lions squad to tour Australia, bearing out Harry Womersley's confidence that he could come into contention for international selection.

However, on 13 December, Roy Francis, the former coach at Leeds and Hull FC who had moved to Australia to coach the North Sydney Bears, watched Jim play against Leeds. Roy spoke to Jim after the game and asked him to consider a move to Sydney on an extended contract. Jim was interested because it would mean a substantial pay rise. However, he would have to find a way to leave Odsal without causing a stir. Jim suggested to Harry Womersley that he was thinking of returning to Wales for personal reasons. Jim mentioned the chance he had of playing in Australia and Harry said he would help Jim sort out his problems. Unfortunately, the national newspapers heard a rumour and printed headlines such as 'Mills may quit Northern'.

Jim recalls: "I had another word with Harry Womersley and told him about the North Sydney offer. Harry said that he would talk to Jack Fricker and see what North Sydney would consider a reasonable fee for me and come back to me. Also about this time I was told that I had been selected for the 1970 tour of Australia and New Zealand with Frank Myler as captain and John Whiteley as coach. This complicated my move to North Sydney. I had spoken about this possible problem to Roy Francis when he initially approached me, but Roy suggested that I could go to North Sydney, play there, come home and still make the

1974 tour. It sounded like good advice at the time, also I was skint.

I decided to go as my domestic problems were still there and to get away for a few years to sort things out. But this was the second big mistake in my career. Who knows, I may have made the British Lions rugby union side if I had stayed in Wales in 1964, now I made another blunder by going to Australia to play for North Sydney instead of going as a Great Britain tourist. And that team were the last one to win the Ashes.

The moment I had confirmation of the transfer to North Sydney, the touring team was published in the press. With sincere apologies both Bradford Northern and I contacted Jack Harding of Leigh, the tourists' team manager, John Whiteley the coach and the RFL to explain that my deal had been agreed. The apology was accepted but I still wonder how things may have been had I toured in 1970.

I played for Bradford Northern until I had to leave for Australia and it was a very enjoyable experience. I had some great times on the field with Tony Fisher and Frank Foster and admired their determination. The crack was always good between us. In one match Tony was caught awkwardly and was flat on his back gasping for breath. I looked down at him lying there and couldn't resist saying: 'I thought you were a champion boxer; what are you doing lying there?' Needless to say Tony growled something unprintable at me and got to his feet."

In his second season at Odsal, Jim played every game for the first 31 matches of the season before leaving with Roy Francis for Australia. He was only sent off once in his time at Bradford, at Belle Vue against Wakefield Trinity for a rough tackle. However, the disciplinary committee found 'sending off sufficient' so Jim was not suspended.

So after two relatively successful seasons at Odsal, Jim was off to a new challenge in Australia.

5. Down under: North Sydney

So, towards the end of the 1969–70 season, probably his most consistent in rugby league, and now aged 25, Jim flew out to Australia, not with the British Lions as a tourist, but to play in the New South Wales Rugby League for North Sydney.

Today, the Australian NRL is clearly overall of a higher standard to Super League. A small number of players move from the British game to play in Australia. But in 1970 the difference was not so pronounced. The Australians had had the better of recent Ashes series, but a number of British players moved to play in Australia in the 1960s, including Dave Bolton, Dick Huddart and Tommy Bishop. Jim outlines that "I found the game a lot faster in Australia. The grounds were a lot firmer, which made the game faster, but I believe that at that time the footballers (ball handlers) were far superior in England. The tackling in Australia was more physical and there were more players in a tackle. When the 1970 tourists beat the Australians to take the Ashes, it was their football that overcame the pace of the Australians. I feel that is why today we are playing the Australian game with so many Australian coaches in the UK."

North Sydney was one of the Australian 'foundation' clubs who established the league in 1908. Their best period was in the early 1920s, when they won the title twice. Australian rugby league historian Sean Fagan succinctly says in his book *The Premiership Clubs* that North Sydney "At best ... had 18 months through 1921 and '22 as the premier Rugby League club in Australia. The rest is a sad tale of underachievement, missed opportunity and downright bad luck."

Andrew Moore, in his social history of the club, *The Mighty Bears!*, argues that the building of the Sydney Harbour Bridge in 1932 started the club's gradual decline which ended in an ill-fated merger with Manly in 1999. The links that North Sydney now had to the rest of the city; and destruction of working class areas in North Sydney over the years saw a fall in support for the club, maybe similar to the process that saw Hunslet collapse in 1973.

Norths' British coach, Roy Francis, was a Welshman of West Indian origin, and was the first black player to play for Great Britain when he faced New Zealand in 1947. He also was capped five times by Wales, and had a successful career before and after the Second World War.

He had a successful coaching record with Hull and Leeds, although his arrival at North Sydney in 1969 was controversial, with current captain-coach, the South African Colin Greenwood resigning and claiming to have been forced out. Francis also had a difficult relationship with the press, particularly after a disastrous defeat against St George in April 1970, which was also Jim's debut.

Roy Francis's contribution to the development of modern rugby league is often overlooked. His experience in the war, working with injured soldiers, had taught him much about motivation. Robert Gate comments in *Gone North* that Francis "became interested in psychology and the way individuals were motivated and realised that to get the most out of a player knowledge of his mental make-up was as crucial as perfecting his physical skills." Francis also believed that all his players, not just the backs, needed pace.

Gate outlines that "His philosophy was that a rugby pitch was up to 75 yards wide and the most effective way to play rugby was to use its width constantly stretching the opposition until it cracked at some point. To cover the width of the pitch he needed 13 athletes not six forwards and seven backs. ...the forwards ... were players like the backs who should be able to run and pass accordingly. There was no place for the ponderous forward who merely lumbered from scrum to scrum." Writing in 1986, Gate outlined that "It is this athleticism permeating modern Australian and New Zealand teams that helps to distinguish them from their British counterparts." He concludes that "In a very real way Roy Francis helped revolutionise the Australian game to the point where it now seems as if they are light years ahead in fitness and motivational techniques." Jim recalls "sprinting sessions at training. Roy had a stop watch, and we had to improve our times. He also worked on our football skills. I didn't do weights seriously until I got to Widnes with Vince Karalius."

Jim says that Francis was "a coach in the Vince Karalius mould, very forward thinking. He brought a lot of things into the game that the Australians are using today. Jack Gibson, the great Australian coach would ring Roy every week and talk about the teams in the league and tactics. When Roy put the phone down, he would say to me 'he's picking my brains', with a smile on his face. Roy had a hard time in Australia with the press and it became too hard to do the job, so in the end he went home, but I'm sure he left a legacy."

Jim was coming into a club that would be involved in controversy, but not of his making! Ian Collis and Alan Whiticker, in their comprehensive *History of Rugby League Clubs,* outline that: "In the opening match of the 1970 season [on 29 March] against Canterbury... Francis instructed his captain, Ken Irvine, to bring his team from the field after he and team-mate John McDonnell had been sent off. The walk-off, which was eventually stopped by official [Harry] 'Akka' Forbes, was a public relations nightmare for the club, but worse was to follow. When Irvine and Francis had a falling-out at the end of the season, the club opted to support their coach, and Irvine, the greatest player the club produced, moved to Manly... Francis returned to England in 1971. Merv Hicks, a tough Welsh prop forward whom Francis had brought to Norths, took over as captain-coach."

Andrew Moore comments that "At the 1970 annual general meeting some North Sydney RLFC members expressed their misgivings about the amount of money that had been spent to so little effect. By January and February 1971, after two mediocre seasons, many club officials also began to feel restive about their messiah. Some complained that he had run riot with the club chequebook, spending some $200,000 on players of questionable value. This was unfair. While it was true that Francis brought the temperamental Jim Mills to North Sydney as well as some utterly forgettable Englishmen, others had been inspired purchases – and cheap ones too. Graham Williams, a smart halfback... had been acquired for... $4302.80."

Jim recalls: "So, having sorted out my family situation in Halifax, I was all set to start a new life in Australia. Roy Francis and his wife had taken an extended close season holiday here in the United Kingdom and Roy was took in a trip to America on his way back to Sydney for the coming season. I travelled on my own to Australia, and had a week in Hawaii on the way to Sydney. I arrived there in early April. To make it easier to enter Australia and for the tax and financial details involved in signing for The Bears, I officially 'emigrated' there." This was the normal procedure for players going to play on long-term contracts, and British citizens going to work in Australia; but Jim is quick to stress that he never became an Australian citizen, and retained his British passport and nationality.

"I lodged with a widow, Mrs Paul, along with a young North Sydney player, Kerry Collien. It was next door to Roy Francis's house, so I spent most of my time with Roy and his wife Renée, who was a lovely lady, as was Mrs Paul.

Training at the North Sydney Oval was very different to what I had done before in league or union. It was a hard, extended time of running. Roy Francis believed that the game was about speed of thought and action, running, then more running. We had, like most Sydney clubs, a trainer. His job was to warm up the squad and put the players through a series of speed, stamina and skills drills which really taxed the most committed players in the squad."

Jim made his debut in Norths' fourth match of the season, at home to St George. The team had lost their first three matches of the season, and the previous week had let in 38 points against Balmain. The *Sydney Morning Herald* commented before the match: "A point of interest will be the performance of North's new buy, massive prop Jim Mills. Mills will be given one of the toughest introductions possible to Sydney football, opposed to Saints' teak-tough John Wittenberg, one of the form props at present."

The match saw another poor display by North Sydney, and a 40–20 defeat, although Jim says that St George "were a top side and very hard". In the *Sun-Herald*, reporter Rod Humphries commented that "North Sydney Bears had their noses rubbed in the dirt... Jim Mills, the costly English import, was there somewhere but did not make any impression in his first game. One could not expect too much after only a week in Sydney." (Australian newspapers often used 'English' instead of 'British' at this time.) Roy Francis said that the result was "humiliating". Jim kept his place for the next match, a visit to Manly. The match report commented: "... Jim Mills was an asset in the first half as he brushed aside would-be tacklers and did plenty of tackling himself. But he tired in the last half hour." Manly scored 16 points in 10 minutes near the end to win 22–13.

Jim's first win for his new side came against Cronulla, whose player-coach was former Great Britain international Tommy Bishop. By now he was getting accustomed to the game in Australia and playing for his new side. Rod Humphries in the *Sun-Herald* reported that "...Jim Mills, although still playing in bursts, is a hard man to put down and he bumped the opposition off like files in some of his runs. He will be a great asset to Norths when he can play the full 80 minutes."

However, Jim recalls: "Tommy Bishop had described me as a

'plodder' in a newspaper article when I arrived. He had never played against me, and his team paid the price when I played against them. I had a blinder, scored a try, made another and put myself about on defence. It was my first really good game in Australia, and Roy Francis said afterwards 'now they know you're here.'"

Jim kept his place in the Norths team, although he missed one match through injury. He scored the winning try four minutes from time in a victory at Parramatta on 31 May, but then on 6 June was sent off, along with three other players, two from each side, against Newtown on 6 June. The *Sydney Morning Herald* reported that "The NSW Rugby League's judiciary committee last night suspended North Sydney prop Jim Mills for two competition matches on a charge of punching and kicking. Three other players sent off in the same incident at North Sydney Oval last Saturday were suspended for one match. They are Oscar Danielson and Phil Flack of Newtown, and Ross Warner of North Sydney. Danielson was ordered off by referee Laurie Bruyeres for punching and tripping. Flack and Warner were charged with punching."

Jim remembers the disciplinary committee in Australia being very different from that at the RFL: "It was like the Old Bailey. Several serious looking men, each with a report of my misdemeanour before them, invited me to sit down. I was surprised by their kindness as they explained that they understood that I may have been targeted and forced into retaliation. The chairman continued 'We would like to think, Mr Mills that you will behave here in Australia as you would in Great Britain and that you will do your utmost to control your temper while playing the game. I appreciate that can be difficult and circumstances could force you into self-defence, but please take this on board, we on this committee do not want you to appear before us again.' Then they gave me a two week ban."

Jim returned to action on 28 June at Balmain, but was in trouble again. He was cautioned for punching Artie Beetson, but then was sent off before half-time "after Balmain skipper Dave Bolton had been flattened in a tackle." Bolton did not come back on for the second half, and Norths lost 29–10. Jim says: "David Bolton was a very good footballer; he sidestepped me twice, was running at me and making a fool of me. I only meant to give him a tap, I did it harder than I meant to and got sent off."

Jim was back before the disciplinary committee, and this time had no excuses. He was given a three match ban. However, he was not back before them until August 1972, just before he finished at North Sydney.

Overall, Jim was sent off three times in first grade matches in Australia, twice in his first season, and once in his third. Myths have grown up around his playing days in Australia, but his disciplinary record was not that bad.

Jim returned to action on 25 July, and played in Norths' last five matches. He scored another try in a 30–7 home win over Parramatta, and the report of Norths' last match of the season, a 15–11 win at Newtown, said that "Norths' forwards, particularly Peter Jacques, Jim Mills and Dave Bridgewater, had a big part in their side's win."

Norths finished the season in ninth place, with seven wins and a draw from their 22 matches. Jim played in six of the seven wins. The report on the season in E.E. Christensen's *Rugby League Year Book* says that although Norths scored 68 tries, which was probably a record for the club, "Penalties proved costly for Norths who had 153 awarded them and 263 against and this situation, coupled with frequent injuries to key players, affected the club's results. In no game did Norths field the same side as in the previous match and injuries to 22 contract players meant their missing a total of 147 first and reserve grade games."

Jim recalls that "We were not a wealthy club in the way that Manly and St George were, but the club had a great deal of spirit and determination. There were some good players at the club when I joined them. The wingers were George Ambrum, who had a spell at Bradford Northern and married on the club's cheerleaders, and another fine international, Ken Irvine. He was our superstar, but he had disagreements with Roy Francis and left to join Manly. Roy was criticised in the press about that.

In the pack was Noel Cavanagh, a good second-rower, who had played with me at Bradford. There was also Phil Franks, a classy stand-off who had started with Penrith, joined Norths in 1971 then moved on to Western Suburbs, and John McDonnell at loose-forward. At hooker was my mate Ross Warner, who was one hard lad. Peter Mullins came with me to Australia after playing with Dewsbury and at Odsal. Graham Williams, who had played for Swinton, was a very good player, and did well for us. It was a big blow when he moved to Manly in 1971. Norths had some good players, but were not a strong side. Roy told me that they were going to be a good side when he signed me."

When he arrived in Australia, Jim was interviewed on television by Ron Casey, who had criticized Roy Francis. Jim spoke about the Great Britain team, and how he felt about joining North Sydney.

Jim played against some quality opposition during his time at Norths: "One of the best forwards was the brilliant footballer and tough bloke, Arthur Beetson who was with Balmain and then Eastern Suburbs. He was a strong, bulky type of forward who would run at a gap and as the tacklers hit him he would half-turn, set himself on strong legs and pass to supporting players. He was a master at this type of play. I had one or two skirmishes with Arthur and I feel there was a mutual admiration between the pair of us. Graeme Langlands was a wonderful player with a great side step, real top-class. John O'Neill was a very good prop for Souths; also at Souths was Ron Coote at loose-forwards, a big, sturdy forward who got about the field very well and Bob McCarthy, a strong-running second-row. At Manly, Bobby Fulton was there along with Malcolm Reilly and Phil Lowe, another strong pack. The game in Australia, just as over here, was a hard slog and I earned my match fee and contract money in every game. I was a target for some of the forwards, having turned down a tour place."

Jim had finished his first season with Norths having played 13 matches and scored three tries. He had missed one match through injury and five through two suspensions.

In 1971, there was a change of coach, as Jim recalls: "The coach who took me to Australia, Roy Francis, departed back to the UK and who took his place as player-coach but my old mate Mervyn Hicks."

Hicks had come to Australia in 1966, having been capped by Great Britain while playing for St Helens. Whiticker and Hudson describe him as an "aggressive force" on the field. He made 78 appearances for Canterbury-Bankstown and had planned to join Norths in 1970, but had to play a final season for Canterbury after a contractual dispute. He stayed at Norths for two seasons as captain-coach, and made 19 first grade appearances. In 1971, he only played six matches, having missed the start of the season with a broken arm, which he then broke again when he returned to action. Control of team selection returned to the club's committee.

In Jim's second season with the club, 1971, he made 17 first grade appearances, and scored four tries. The season started disastrously, with a 42–3 defeat at Cronulla. But in the next match, at home to Wests, Jim scored a try in a 21–16 win, and the *Sun-Herald* reported that "It was a good performance by Norths who showed a new spirit." After another heavy defeat, at Parramatta, Norths beat Canterbury 17–10. The *Sun-Herald* commented that: "Norths' big prop, Jim Mills, and second-rowers Bruce Walker and Peter Jacques paved the way for victory."

Jim only missed five matches this season. He was injured for a couple of games in May, when Merv Hicks came into the team at prop, and missed three towards the end of the season through injury with a torn hamstring. After a narrow defeat at Wests on 20 June, the *Sydney Morning Herald* reported that: "Led by giant prop Jim Mills and five-eighth Mal McLachlan, [Norths] levelled the score at 17-all with 10 minutes play remaining." A penalty near the end saw another loss. A couple of days later, Graham Williams was transferred to Manly, which was a major setback for Norths.

Often the team would do well in the first half, but run out of steam after the break. There were a couple of major defeats before the end of the season, and after a 48–5 hammering at Manly, five players were dropped. Before Jim's final match of the season, against Souths, the *Herald* commented: "Although Norths' form is nothing to rave about, their big pack of forwards, headed by Englishman Jim Mills and experienced hooker Ross Warner, will make it tough for Souths." Jim was injured in a 40–7 defeat, and the team finished 11th, one place off the bottom, with just five wins and a draw.

However, in his third season, 1972, Jim only played for the first grade side seven times, and scored just one try. Moore outlines that "In his final year for Norths he played more games in reserves than in firsts and was twice picked in third grade." Jim recalls that this was for "disciplinary reasons". Some of his absence from the first team was explained by a phone call he got in early June. It was terrible news – his uncle was phoning to say that his brother David had been killed in a road accident. Jim was hit hard by this, and recalls that he did not play for a few weeks.

Jim missed the first four first team matches of the season, and then played against Newtown on 22 April at the Sydney Cricket Ground. The match was designated the 'match of the day' and played on the Saturday. Norths were 21–11 up, but had to be satisfied with a draw. Jim scored one of their tries. He kept his place for a couple of matches, an Anzac day defeat against Souths, and a 39–10 drubbing at Wests, when he was injured. His next match was against Manly on 28 May, and he kept his place the following week in a narrow win over Cronulla. He then lost his place to Merv Hicks, who was himself dropped by the club selectors in June. Jim returned to the first team on 6 August, in a narrow loss to Easts. His final game for North Sydney was against Canterbury on 13 August, He was sent off by referee Richie Humphrey and was given a four match suspension by the disciplinary committee, so missed Norths' final game at Manly. Overall, Norths improved slightly in 1972, ending with seven wins and a draw from their 22 matches.

Jim played in 37 first grade matches out of 66 while he was at Norths. However, in his first season he missed the first three matches as he only arrived in Sydney in early April, so played 13 out of the 19 matches for which he was available. In his second season, he played 17 matches out of 22, missing five through injury. So in his first two seasons, he played in 30 out of 41 possible first grade matches. He was also often praised in the press. It was only in his third season when he did not make so much impact, and even then missed three matches through injury. By then, he was looking forward to going home. And he was always playing in a struggling team.

Looking back, he says that the game there was "massive" compared to Great Britain, and playing on hard grounds he had to be fitter. He enjoyed his time there and "made some great friends."

Andrew Moore found Jim's time in Sydney disappointing, saying that "... the problem with big Jim was not his speed or lack of it; on occasions in fact he displayed a sprightly turn of acceleration for a 17-stone man. On a football field it was Jim Mills's temper that made him a disappointment." However, certainly for Jim's two first seasons, match reports at the time do not support this view.

Jim's disciplinary record when he arrived in Australia was not that bad – he had only been sent off three times in England. But it was known that he had turned down a place on the Lions tour to play for North Sydney, and with his size, and being regarded as "English (!)" he was clearly a target for the 'enforcers' from other teams.

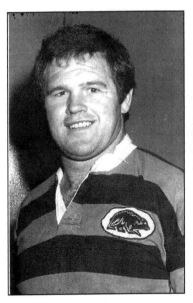

Left: A Welshman down under: Jim in a North Sydney shirt. (Courtesy *Rugby League Journal*)
Right: At home in North Sydney, 1971.

In 1971, British rugby league legend Mal Reilly was a big signing for Manly. In his autobiography, he recalls that "I had arrived with something of a reputation and everyone was hell-bent on fixing me up. The game was survival, a matter of looking after yourself... Looking back now [1999] some of the things that went on in those days make me shudder." Reilly was sent off twice in his first few weeks in Sydney. No doubt the welcome for Jim was similar. However, Reilly was a very different player from Jim; and maybe was more pro-actively 'hard' whereas Jim tended to react to situations that developed during matches.

Moore says that Jim played 37 "spiteful" games for North Sydney, but the game itself in Australia at the time was pretty violent, to say the least. A year after Jim left Australia – so it was nothing to do with him – the 1973 Grand Final was the most violent ever. Alan Clarkson described it as "the most vicious grand final in years" and Malcolm Andrews comments that if he had replaced "years" with "in the history of the game", no one would have argued. Maybe Jim didn't make as big an impact as North Sydney hoped, although the coach who had brought him to the club left after his first season, and Norths were always a struggling side; but it is hard to conclude that his style of play at the time was so different from the names that fill Malcolm Andrews's book from that period.

48

When he arrived in Australia, Jim worked with George Ambrum at a wastepaper company. They collected wastepaper from shops, and sorted it. For his last few months he worked as a doorman at a hotel in Cremorne and, according to Moore, "enjoyed a harum-scarum existence both on and off the field." It can be argued that Moore's comment is not really justified. Jim recalls: "There were a few bits of trouble. One night there were about six lads making trouble. I went over, tapped the biggest one on the shoulder and said 'behave or its time to go'. He said 'step outside'. We went out down a long corridor and he was rolling his sleeves up. I knocked him out in a few seconds, and said to his mates to take him home. About 50 people were watching. But Harry McKinnon spoke to me and said the club could get a bad name, so I packed it in."

It is fair to say that Jim was involved in some escapades during his time in Sydney: "I linked up with another Welshman, Mervyn Hicks. Mervyn and I used to paint the town red regularly and because he was almost as big as me we never had much trouble even in the tough areas such as the docks. Except for once; there was a big bar which had an early form of Karaoke. Everyone was singing and enjoying ourselves. Someone bumped in to Mervyn, and knocked his beer. He said 'watch where you're going'. Punches were thrown, and the two of us, along with Johnny Payne, another North Sydney forward, ended up in the street with about a dozen others. We got away, but because we were known as rugby players word got back to North Sydney.

The North Sydney president was Harry McKinnon and a nice bloke. He was a former player, a second-rower, and his son, Don McKinnon toured with the 1982 'Invincibles'. He spoke to us and we told him we didn't start the trouble. He told us to keep out of places like that."

Another time, I was in the North Sydney Leagues Club and I called the barman. He ignored me, and said something to me 'Pommie...' I was having a drink with former Australian forward Noel Kelly, who said 'take no notice'. The barman put my change halfway down the bar. He came out from behind the bar; I met him halfway and flattened him. Eric Dawson, the manager of the Leagues Club, asked me to leave. I had to go in front of the board and admitted I was out of order and shouldn't have hit him. If they hadn't done anything the union would have taken the staff out on strike and closed the club. I was banned from the club for a few months. Obviously I had been out of line.

The spell in Australia helped build up my finances and I had a trip home every close season in my contract. This was vital as it allowed me to see my family every six months. Having my family so far away was a pain and possibly that was one of the reasons why I was lost my rag so quickly and was sent off on occasions while playing in Australia."

Jim was offered the chance to stay at Norths: "Not long into my third season for North Sydney, the directors offered me another year's contract. This would have meant that I would have played four seasons away from home. The main reason for me going down under in the first place was to strengthen my financial standing and this I did. But that third season at North Sydney, while it was great the way they looked after me, had me wanting to go back home more so every week that passed. I explained my feelings to Mervyn and he had a word with Harry McKinnon and it was decided to let me go back to the UK."

Looking back, Jim says that "Malcolm Reilly, Phil Lowe and Cliff Watson all went on the 1970 Lions tour, and then signed for Sydney clubs. I could have done that. I should have gone on the 1970 tour, then gone to Australia. When I played there, I had some good games, but was inconsistent." By 1975, when a short-term contract after the World Championship was a possibility, Jim says he "was much fitter, and a different player."

Jim made some good friends in North Sydney. But at the end of the 1972 season, it was time to return home. The best years of his rugby league career were about to begin.

6. Back home: Widnes 1972 to 1976

Through no fault of his own, Jim's move from North Sydney back to an English club was complicated and controversial. In December 1971, the Australian rugby league player Dennis Tutty won a case in the Australian High Court against the NSWRL and his club, Balmain, over the club's right to retain his registration once his contract had ended. The legal argument was similar to that put forward by George Eastham, an England international footballer, in the British courts in 1963. So, under that ruling, Jim should have been able to join any club of his choosing once his contract with North Sydney was up.

However, his case also became entangled in the latest ruling on British and Australasian players being able to play in Australia or Great Britain respectively. Almost since the sport became established in Australia and New Zealand, the authorities on both sides of the globe had introduced international transfer bans or restrictions on players' movements from one side of the globe to the other by using residence qualifications. There were various reasons behind this – it gave the clubs more control over their players; it stopped all the league competitions being destabilised by large numbers of players moving around the globe, and provided stability for international matches and tours. The New Zealand situation was slightly different because their domestic competition until the mid–1980s was amateur. Another outcome of the bans was that international rugby union players could be recruited, but not league players. It also led to large scale recruitment of South African union players, particularly in the 1920s and late 1950s to mid–1960s. Welsh or Scottish union players, of course, could join British rugby league clubs at any time, and it was very rare for a player to be recruited by an Australian rugby league club direct from British rugby union

The latest attempt to control this phenomenon was a one year residence qualification for British or Australian players to play in Australia or Great Britain respectively. Jim had 'emigrated' to Australia when he joined North Sydney, although he remained a British citizen. Did he now have to serve a residence qualification?

From contemporary reports of the saga, it appears that Jim's contract with North Sydney ran until March 1973 – he had signed for three years in March 1970. On 8 November, the *Rugby Leaguer* reported that "North Sydney forward Jim Mills, who has been unable to join Halifax owing to his club requesting a £3,000 fee for only five months could – if his solicitor prevents Norths holding their player while he is in this country – become a Widnes player. He may stay here as he feels a player can now earn as much in Britain with a successful side. Mills watched the Warrington-Widnes BBC2 Floodlit first round match at Wilderspool last week, and then had a drink with his friend John Warlow, Widnes's open side prop."

In October, it had been reported that Jim was expected to join Halifax, but then on 25 October 1972, the *Leaguer* reported that the club's "Supporters and officials are disappointed that Jim Mills is unlikely to play with Halifax, who now appear to be fourth in line for his services."

Jim made his debut for Widnes in the reply of the BBC2 Floodlit Trophy tie against Warrington on 14 November 1972. On 6 December, the *Leaguer* reported, under the headline 'transfer deals will continue' that "Prop Jim Mills, now playing with Widnes, says he won a court action to establish that he is now a free agent and that his club, North Sydney, are not entitled to the £4,000 transfer fee they are asking. League officials here have granted him a provisional clearance to play with the Chemics, but quite obviously they are not happy with the situation. On the face of it, his move to Widnes is a direct breach of the new law and inquiries are being made with Australia to confirm the legal position."

However, the Australians were not satisfied. In June 1975, after playing for Wales in the World Championship in Australia, Jim was considering a short-term deal to play for Canterbury-Bankstown or Manly-Warringah. However, at an International Board meeting later the same month, ARL president Kevin Humphreys said that the fee was still outstanding, and threatened that unless the matter resolved, Jim would not be able to sign for a Sydney club, and the Australians would not pay fees to British clubs for future transfers. This clearly alarmed the RFL, who paid the outstanding $4,000 fee to Norths and said that they would recover the money from Widnes.

Jim reflects on his return home in 1972: "When I arrived back home I went to my mam's house. I visited Halifax to see my kids and did the rounds to see my old mates. The season in Australia was almost at an end. I had signed a three season contract with North Sydney and although they wanted me to sign another one year deal I had not signed anything. So I had done my three seasons and was, I thought, a free agent. I contacted North Sydney and told them this, but they said I was still a North Sydney player and they would let me talk to any English club about a transfer, but would expect a transfer fee for my services.

The fee they wanted was $3,000 (£1,700), a large sum in those days for the rest of my contract. [The British record transfer fee in 1972–73 was £13,500]. As soon as I arrived home Halifax club contacted me to ask if I would play for them. Bradford Northern also wanted me back at Odsal, but both moves were stopped by the fee to North Sydney. Nevertheless, three clubs came in for me, Wigan, Bradford Northern and Widnes. I was unable to play for anyone until the transfer fee was paid to North Sydney. This had to be sorted out or I could have been frozen out of the game completely. So I ran it past a solicitor, Frank Nyland – who was on the board at Widnes. He got a barrister to look at it and he recommended applying for an injunction against North Sydney, which I did. Widnes came in with their offer to the Australian club and it was accepted. The legalities to sort out this tangle had begun in mid-October 1972 and after a while papers were exchanged between the two sets of lawyers."

What happened from 18 October to 14 November was that Widnes decided that I was the man they wanted, offered a nominal amount, and suddenly a clearance was granted by the RFL which allowed me to play again in this country. However, the RFL were under pressure not to mess up the international agreement. I was 22 stone, overweight, and looked like an all-in wrestler. Vinty had me working on the weights and running round the ploughed fields near his home and got me fit.

I trained with a good amateur boxer from Widnes, Tony Strong, who Vinty has taken under his wing as well. He fought in the ABA finals as a light welterweight. Vinty had a punch-bag hanging from a tree, and we did six three-minute sessions on it.

I went into digs in Widnes with a super couple, Barry and Jean Hynan, and they looked after me in great style, they were smashing to me. The Widnes captain was my old Welsh mate John Warlow. Also at Widnes was George Nicholls who gave tremendous service to the club before his move to St Helens in January 1973. George played with me in the Great Britain pack in the 'Dad's Army' test at Odsal in 1978 and toured with me in 1974 and 1979 for the Lions. George would always take the ball up; you always wanted a forward like him in your side."

Interviewed in 2007, by the *National Rugby League Archive*, Vince Karalius recalled that "I had never seen Jim play. When he first came to the club he was totally unfit. He was huge. He played a couple of games and I thought he would have to improve.

He came to my home for training, and I got him down to 17 stone. He trained with Tony Strong. He had some pace, and a tremendous heart. He could cause havoc; he was a great player and great with the team. He was an imposing figure, but also had a sense of humour. He was like a giant – a huge fellow in every way. But he was well liked in the team, although he would fight at the drop of a hat. I needed my man management skills with him at times."

Jim made a good decision in signing for Widnes, because the club was on the verge of the greatest period in its history. The club had joined the Northern Union in 1895, but precious few trophies had found their way to Naughton Park. There had been some success in the 1930s, with two Challenge Cup wins and a runners-up spot in the Championship. In 1945–46 the Lancashire Cup was won, but the trophy cabinet was then bare until 1964, when Hull KR were beaten at Wembley.

Widnes now has a population of just over 58,000; and is part of the borough of Halton. The town is between Liverpool and Manchester, and the club were – before Super League – known as the Chemics, reflecting the chemicals industry's role as a major employer in the town. Historically, Widnes was part of Lancashire, but after a local government reorganisation is part of Cheshire.

In the summer of 1971 Widnes had appointed Vince Karalius as first team coach, and given him full control of first team affairs. He would select the team, rather than a committee of directors. It was an appointment that would transform the club. Karalius had made his name as a player at St Helens, and won every honour in the game, including some tremendous performances for Great Britain. In 1962 he had joined Widnes, become team captain for the 1963–64 season and had taken the team to victory at Wembley. As well as being one of the game's most skilful forwards, he was widely recognised as one of the toughest. He was also a fierce motivator, both as a player and a coach.

However, it is interesting that Malcolm Andrews, in *Hardmen*, says that off the pitch "Karalius was a mild-mannered gentleman (in the true sense of the word) and a devout churchgoer, who would sing lullabies to babies and was loved unconditionally by everyone who met him socially." While that description does not exactly apply to Jim, the similarities are interesting – two men with a fierce reputation on the pitch, but very different when not playing rugby league."

Jim recalls: "Vinty was the catalyst behind that great Widnes side. His training techniques were ahead of the other teams; we were fitter and often won matches in the last 20 minutes. We did sessions of weight training, had a weights room with leg machines and freestanding weights. He looked at diets, vitamins and even gave us a glass of sherry before we played sometimes. On training nights, we would sit in the bath and listen to him talking about the game. The water would get cold. When I was there, most of the players were Widnes lads.

Vinty was a great motivator; he was so passionate about the game. He did a wonderful job with me. Things went right for at Widnes. I needed someone like Vinty; I couldn't have gone to a better place. I put all my success there down to him. I have a lot of respect for him."

Jim was recommended to Widnes by Merv Hicks and Graham Williams: "Vinty met them at a function and asked if they knew and good forwards. They said that I was coming home, that I was bigger than Merv, and Graham said he should sign me. I was in Cardiff and he flew down with Widnes chairman Jim Davies. My mam made sandwiches for them. I was getting a few offers, but I was impressed by the way he spoke to me. He said that Widnes would be a great side, but needed a big forward. We agreed terms, I took them to the airport and I knew I was doing the right thing. Before my debut, I went to the first match against Warrington in the BBC2 Floodlit Trophy. At half-time I went into the dressing room and Vinty introduced me to the other players: 'This is Jim Mills. He's signed for us. Look at the size of him.'"

Vince Karalius's first season at Widnes saw some success, with an appearance in the Lancashire Cup Final. He had inherited some promising local youngsters, and reinforced them with some shrewd signings, including Jim, and five months later Doug Laughton, who soon became the team captain.

Widnes beat Warrington 14–11 on Jim's debut. He recalls being very overweight at the time, but Karalius kept faith with him and got Jim down to his best playing weight, just under 18 stones. Widnes beat Leeds and Wakefield to reach their first final in the BBC2 Floodlit Trophy. Jim missed the semi-final against Wakefield, but was a regular member of the team and won his place back before the final.

They faced Leigh, who were coached by Les Pearce – Jim's old friend from Halifax – at Wigan's Central Park on 19 December. It was also Jim's first final in rugby league, but he only lasted six minutes. An early clash with Leigh forward Geoff Fletcher saw Leigh prop Paul Grimes get involved, and both props were sent off by referee Fred Lindop. The *John Player Rugby League Yearbook* reported that: "Following a crunching tackle by Mills on Fletcher... Grimes, it seemed, paid the penalty for joining in the fracas, for it was he and Mills who received marching orders while Fletcher was allowed to remain on the field to become a vital cog in Leigh's forward supremacy." Jim says that "I was trying to put Fletcher off his game, he was their ballplayer and I knocked him to the ground. It wold have been ok, but Grimes came in swinging punches and I defended myself. It was my first final and my mum and dad were watching on television in Wales. I was sick as a pig. I thought it was a bad decision to send us off, no one was hurt. He could have ruined the game, sending two off early in a final. He could have been more lenient." A second half try from Graham Lawson, followed by a penalty by Jimmy Fiddler gave Leigh a 5–0 victory.

Jim was banned for two matches, but by the end of the season had made 22 appearances for Widnes, and scored five tries, his best ever tally in a season at that time. Widnes finished the season in 12th place in the league, and lost 33–6 to Wakefield Trinity in the first round of the play-offs.

This season built the base for further success. Jim recalls that "John Warlow was coming to the end of his career. But there were a lot of good young Widnes lads coming through." Ray Dutton was at full-back, but Keith Ewell, Mick Adams, Bob Blackwood, Reg Bowden and Mick George all became first team regulars. Jim also says that Doug Laughton was an important signing: "he was a great footballer with a lot of experience. He was a good passer. It was sad to see George Nicholls go [in January 1973] but he won plenty at St Helens."

In 1973–74 Lancashire clubs won all the major trophies except one, the BBC2 Floodlit Trophy, which saw little Bramley win the only trophy in their history. Salford won the First Division, and it was Widnes's local rivals Warrington who dominated in the cup competitions, winning four. The league had been split into two divisions, and Widnes were more consistent than in 1972–73, and finished fourth, with 18 wins and a draw from 30 matches. Jim made 27 first team appearances, plus one from the bench. He was sent off just once – against Leigh on 24 February 1974 for tripping – but 'sending off sufficient' was the decision of the disciplinary committee, so he was not suspended.

The team's only appearance in a final came in the BBC2 Floodlit Trophy. Wins at Leigh and Salford saw Widnes into the semi-final, where they achieved a 13–8 win away to Hull KR. Predictions before the semi-finals would have been for a Lancashire derby in the final. Hull KR were struggling near the bottom of the First Division, and Bramley, who faced St Helens, eventually finished just clear of the relegation zone. But Bramley won 13–12 against the Saints, and faced Widnes at Naughton Park on December 18. Nine days earlier, Widnes had won the league match at Naughton Park between the two teams 27–6.

The match was played in daylight because of restrictions on floodlit sport due to the miners' strike. Bramley took the lead in the third minute and never looked back. Vince Karalius admitted that his side was "well-licked". Bramley were 5–4 up at half-time and won 15–7. Jim missed the final because he was suspended.

Two of the players who went on to play major roles for Widnes in their period as the sport's 'Cup Kings' became established this season – scrum-half Reg Bowden made 41 appearances, and Mick Adams 24.

Jim's success on the pitch was recognised by the Great Britain selectors. He had not been selected for any of the five test matches during the season against France and Australia, but made 15 starts on the Lions tour, plus appearance from the bench, and played in three tests.

The frustrations of 1973–74 were forgotten in 1974–75. The Challenge Cup Final victory over Warrington was the culmination of a successful season, and the team's third cup final appearance. On the way to Wembley, Widnes faced Second Division opposition in the first three rounds. But in those days, all teams were part-time players, and there was not the huge gulf between the top flight and second tier that there is in today's game. Widnes won 13–4 at Swinton, by a point at Hull and then 10–4 at Oldham, when the *Leaguer* reported that "Oldham fought magnificently... It was the try and the surging runs of Doug Laughton and Jim Mills which finally broke them." In the semi-final, Widnes overcame Wakefield Trinity 13–7 at Odsal. The Leaguer said that Jim "rocked Trinity with his powerful second half bursts."

In the league, Widnes dropped a place to fifth, but with the same number of points as in 1973–74. The season's first success came in the Lancashire Cup. Wins against Oldham, Rochdale – after a replay – and Leigh saw Widnes face Salford in the final at Central Park on 2 November. A penalty by Ray Dutton put Widnes ahead at half-time, Mick George added a try, and a drop-goal from Eric Hughes sealed a close-fought 6–2 win.

The *John Player Rugby League Yearbook* reported that Widnes's "backs showed plenty of resolve – if not much spectacular play – but it was on their forwards that Widnes leaned most heavily. Mills, Elwell, Stephens, Adams, Blackwood and Laughton did everything asked of them." It was the first time Widnes had won the Cup since 1945.

Nearly three months later, Widnes played their second final of the season, this time in the Player's No.6 Trophy. Victories over Featherstone Rovers, Wakefield Trinity and Swinton saw the Chemics into the semi-final, where they beat Hull KR 16–14 at Naughton Park. Three weeks later, they faced Jim's old club Bradford Northern in "atrocious conditions" at Warrington's Wilderspool Stadium. Widnes were favourites, but a try by Bradford's Stuart Carlton in the first half won the game for them.

Widnes's only reply came from a penalty by Dutton. The report in the *John Player Rugby League Yearbook* said that the Bradford forwards "were particularly effective in blunting the fearsome, hard-to-hold charges of Widnes prop forward Jim Mills".

In the *Rugby Leaguer's* preview of the Final, Bob Myers wrote that: "Up front, big Jim Mills is running like a tank these days, and given that he can curb his impetuosity, will be a major weapon in attack..." The paper's report on the match said that Widnes lost "...despite the mighty runs of Jim Mills..."

Winning the Lancashire Cup in 1974–75. Jim with Bob Blackwood,
Mick Adams and Ray Dutton.

Missed! Bradford Northern's Nigel Stephenson tries to stop Jim.

Wembley 1975

Every player fortunate enough to play in a Challenge Cup Final will always remember their first appearance at Wembley; especially if they are on the winning side. Jim played in 14 finals in different competitions in eight years during his time with Widnes, and represented Great Britain and Wales, but the highlight of Jim's 17 year career as a senior rugby player in both codes was playing for Widnes against Warrington at Wembley in 1975.

Jim recalls: "We won 14–7. John Bevan, another former Cardiff rugby union player, scored first. I scored a try for Widnes, and we kicked the goals that gave us victory. It was a great occasion, all my family were at Wembley, which was important for me. We were the better side. Earlier that season we had won the Lancashire Cup, and it was the start of the Cup Kings period for Widnes, and a big point in my career. I ran in from 15 yards to score from a pass by Eric Hughes. I scored at the end where the Widnes fans were. Time stopped – as I touched down I became aware of the crowd rising up to celebrate.

It was the first time I had played at Wembley. I had been to the previous two finals as a fan, with John Warlow and Kel Coslett.

The whole cup final experience was all new to me. We went round the ground the day before. We stayed at a hotel in St Albans. I remember in the changing rooms everyone was quiet before the game, and I tried to encourage people.

Vince Karalius was our coach, and Alex Murphy was coaching Warrington. Neither had lost at Wembley, so one of them would lose their unbeaten record. Vince told us when we were in the tunnel waiting to go out to look straight ahead, and not talk to them. I knew a lot of their team, but Vince said that we were to be like soldiers, focussed and professional. I never doubted that we would win.

We were the better side on the day. I will always remember walking up the steps to receive the cup and our medals from Princess Alexandra and the celebrations in the dressing room afterwards. I was interviewed by Frank Bough about my try at the end of the game, and told him that I had 'done three sidesteps'. Bough asked David Watkins about this afterwards, and David told him that I was pulling his leg.

That evening we had a great celebration at the hotel, and I remember going to the station to see off the fans who were going home by train. It was the first really big game I played in."

Rugby league historian Les Hoole wrote that "Led superbly by their forwards, Widnes gradually took command of the game with their particular brand of controlled and methodical football." Ray Dutton had kicked two penalties to make the score 5–4 to Warrington before Jim scored. Dutton also converted Jim's try and kicked a further penalty to see Widnes ahead 11–5 at half-time. Warrington pulled back two points with a penalty, but a further penalty and drop goal near the end by Dutton made the final score 14–7. Warrington had been favourites to retain the cup, and Hoole says that "the little underdogs from Widnes had pulled off a major Wembley upset and done it in style." Ray Dutton won the Lance Todd Trophy for man-of-the-match.

Jack Winstanley wrote in the *1975–76 John Player Rugby League Yearbook* that "The score of 14–7 in Widnes's favour did not do them full justice... Overall, the picture of this final, well worth the remembering, was of an ultra-fit, determined Widnes side with a killer streak running through its core, against a Warrington outfit that, with a few exceptions looked strangely lethargic..." He also quotes Vince Karalius as saying uncompromisingly "We murdered them, we were too fast and too fit for them." The caption of the photo of Jim with the report said that his try "was just one triumph for this rugged Welshman: the other was keeping his cool and remaining on the field for the whole of the game."

Four against one: Jim charges forward against Warrington at Wembley, as Reg Bowden watches. (Photo: Aaron Photography)

Bursting through to score against Warrington at Wembley, 1975.

1975 Challenge Cup Final: Alan Prescott and Keith Elwell congratulate Jim on scoring the winning try for Widnes.
(Courtesy *Rugby League Journal*)

Top: Celebrating.
Middle: The centre of attention with Vince Karalius.
Bottom: With Vince Karalius and the Cup.

Jim holds the Cup aloft in front on jubilant Widnes supporters.
(Photo: Aaron Photography)

Mick George became a regular player for Widnes this season, and another newcomer was Australian winger Chris Anderson, who made 19 appearances. Jim made 35 first team appearances; his best ever in a season, and scored five tries. He was sent off once, against Rochdale Hornets on 13 September 1974 for a 'vicious shoulder charge and kicking' for which he was banned for two matches, and was given two cautions on 27 February 1975, which were treated as a dismissal, and resulted in a one match ban.

Problems with the disciplinary committee were starting to affect Jim's game. On 12 March, the *Leaguer* reported that "Widnes prop Jim Mills may quit the game at the end of the season – because he feels he is being victimised by certain rugby league referees. Matters came to a head for 'Big Jim', a Welsh international, when he was dismissed during the recent England - Wales match at Salford, following an incident with England forward Mike Coulman. 'I've been given the bad boy image, which I don't deserve', he said. 'Some coaches are telling their players to get me off. Referees are penalising me because of my physical strength.'

Mills is due to appear before the disciplinary committee at the end of the month. Whatever his decision on the future, Jim had made it clear that he will still play for Wales in Australia if selected."

Jim was given a two match ban, and did not miss any of Widnes's Challenge Cup ties. On 2 April, the *Leaguer* reported: "Widnes star prop Jim Mills is all set to face Wakefield Trinity in the Challenge Cup semi-final at Odsal on Saturday. The two match suspension he received last week was accounted for over the Easter period. This is great news for Widnes fans who feared that if 'Big Jim' was given a stiff sentence, he might quit the game altogether. Mills felt he was being victimised by referees, an attitude which was endorsed by one of his admirers, Huyton chairman Wilf Hunt.

Mr Hunt said: 'Mills is a tremendous advertisement for rugby league. Probably the finest prop in the world today. Sell this game of ours, and there can be no finer spectacle than Mills powering his way through the opposition'." Jim remembers that Wilf Hunt "later came onto the board at Widnes. He had played for Huyton, had an engineering company and a restaurant in Widnes. He used to come and watch our matches."

Vince Karalius left at the end of the 1974–75 season, because of business commitments. Frank Myler took over as coach at Widnes: "Frank was a different type of coach. He was good tactically and all the players respected him. The appointment was kept within the club. It was the same as at Liverpool FC at the time – Vinty was followed by Frank Myler who was followed by Doug Laughton. The training methods were still the same. He was a good communicator and did a good job."

The 1975–76 season brought further success for Widnes, and two more cup final appearances for Jim; but events in the World Championship match against New Zealand on 2 November (covered elsewhere in this book) saw him leave Widnes at the end of January 1976.

Once again, the Lancashire Cup provided early season success for Widnes. A victory over Whitehaven was followed by a bye in the second round, and a 16–2 win at Derwent Park over Workington in the semi-final saw Widnes into the final without having played a team from Lancashire. There they faced Salford at Central Park on 4 October, a repeat of the previous season's final. Jim was now a vital part of the Widnes set-up. Previewing the match, the *Leaguer* commented: "Up to last weekend Mills had not played since he aggravated an old knee injury in the opening match of the season at Wigan. Widnes will be relying heavily on Mills to give them the extra power they need to complete the county cup double over Salford and add to their Wembley success earlier this year."

The *John Player Rugby League Yearbook* reported that Widnes built many of their attacks around the forward trio of Mills, Foran and Adams. And a formidable trio it turned out to be..." Widnes took the lead early on, and although Salford were 5–3 during the first half, by half-time Widnes were 8–5 up and won comfortably 16–7.

In the Players No.6 Trophy, Widnes went one better than the previous season, and won it. Jim played in the first round win over Dewsbury and second round win at Wigan, but was suspended for the third round and semi-final, following his sending off while playing for Wales against New Zealand.

The disciplinary committee met on the 10th November, discussed the incident and promptly slapped an eight weeks ban on Jim. In the *Daily Mirror*, Jim commented to reporter Joe Humphreys: "I know what I did was wrong and I deserve to be punished. But his is taking my wages from me – stopping me playing for Widnes."

Widnes believed that because Jim was dismissed in an international match, any suspension should not cover club games. Sumner Baxendale (Wigan), Jack Myerscough (Leeds) and Les Pounder of Wakefield were appointed by the RFL to hear the appeal. Their decision was to increase the ban from eight games to the end of the season. The committee said that they had "sympathy with the Widnes club, but in view of the severity of the offences and the serious injuries sustained by the victim have decided that they suspension on Mills be extended until the end of the current season." Jim commented: "I have not even made an appeal against the suspension myself – this is something the club have done – but I am suffering still more." Jim said that he would take legal advice.

A few days later, the Auckland Rugby League had banned Jim from playing in Auckland. It was also reported that the Wellington Rugby League had asked the New Zealand authorities to impose a complete ban on Jim or any team of which Jim may be a member. Jim commented: "I am beginning to feel I'm being victimised. It doesn't worry me too much about New Zealand, but this sort of publicity is not helpful. I want to get this decision by the Rugby League reversed so I can get back to playing again in the New Year".

Jim took advice, and believed that the RFL had broken its own rules over the appeal. He wasn't represented, and challenged them through the courts. The RFL backed down before the hearing started and the original ban was reinstated. Frank Corless reported in the *Daily Mirror* that "The decision in the Liverpool High Court means that Mills will now be able to play in the new year." Jim was awarded his costs by Mr Justice Payne and Corless said that he had made legal history in his action against the RFL. Jim commented in the *Daily Telegraph* that "It was obvious that the League were wrong. I am happy at winning but upset in a way that I had to go to such lengths to get justice." However, on 18 December it was reported that the New Zealand Rugby League had banned him from playing there. This was not an immediate problem for Jim, but would become an issue in the future.

Back on the pitch, Jim returned to action for Widnes at the beginning of January, his suspension completed. The Player's No.6 Trophy final was against Second Division Hull on 24 January at Headingley. It was to be Jim's last match for Widnes for over a year. Don Yates's preview in the *Rugby Leaguer* said that "Like Hull, [Widnes] have an outstanding pack, which is made even stronger with the return after suspension of Jim Mills."

Jack Winstanley's report said that "...after eight minutes' play, big Jim Mills nonchalantly shrugged off three tackles to send loose-forward Mick Adams racing unopposed to the Hull posts...". Dutton's conversion of Adams's try put Widnes 7–0 up, but by half-time the Humberside

side had fought back to 8–8. With 20 minutes left, Widnes were a point clear, 14–13, but a further try from scrum-half Reg Bowden meant another winner's medal for Jim and a 19–13 win for the Chemics.

Widnes went on to reach the Challenge Cup Final again, but were well beaten, 20–5, by St Helens. Nick Nelson was in Jim's place in the front-row. But Jim had moved to Workington Town, looking for somewhere to play a little less in the limelight after the 'Greengrass incident'. In the final season of his first spell at Widnes, Jim made 10 appearances and scored a try. He was sent off once, against Oldham in the BBC2 Floodlit Trophy on 30 September, for striking, but was found 'not guilty' by the disciplinary committee, the only time this he achieved this result in his British career.

Jim felt that if he stayed at Widnes, playing in the First Division for one of the country's leading sides in high profile matches, he would inevitably be under the spotlight. In early February, he was put on the transfer list by Widnes at £8,000. It was reported that Salford were interested, raising the prospect of a return to a former club, and playing again with a former Welsh team-mate, Colin Dixon.

However, this would not solve the problem of Jim's high profile. A move to a Second Division club allowed him to continue playing. He recalls Workington Town's chairman Tom Mitchell phoning him from Geneva asking him if he was interested in moving to his club. The deal was soon agreed. Part of it was that he would mainly train in Widnes, and only travel to Workington for home matches and training sessions before cup ties.

On 18 February, after Jim had completed his move to Workington, the Widnes correspondent of the *Rugby Leaguer* provided some background to the move. Dave Gregory wrote: "The departure of Big Jim Mills from Naughton Park was a sad event all round, but – as both club and player pointed out – a necessary one. Mills's much-publicised unemployment problem had a lot to do with it, but it wasn't the only reason. [Jim says that this was not an issue in the transfer and that he was working at the time] The 16½ stone Welsh prop-forward was frightened of getting sent off again, especially in a big match.

Soon after signing for Workington Town for the modest fee of £6,250 three days before the Cup deadline, Mills said: 'My three years with Widnes were the most enjoyable of my career. They have a great bunch of lads there, and I'm indebted to Vinty Karalius for getting me fighting-fit after my spell down under. Frank Myler too is a great man to work for, and you couldn't ask for a better set of team-mates. The supporters were also wonderful. They treated me like a hero.' But Mills told me that he had been thinking about the situation for months, and realised it would be fatal for him to lose his temper again, especially when playing for Widnes.

'Workington fit the bill perfectly and I'm looking forward to a successful spell with them.' The Chemics blamed Mills for leaving them no option but to sell him, but Jim said: "I would never have got away unless I had threatened the club." Mills's threat was that he would return to South Wales if they did not grant his transfer request.

So Jim was off to the Lake District, and the challenge of helping Workington win promotion into the First Division. He was now aged 31, but still had much to offer to rugby league.

Workington Town RLFC at Derwent Park in 1976. Back: Ike Southward, Tom Mitchell, I. Gorley, R. Calvin, I. Wright, P. Gorley, Jim, E. Bowman, J. Risman, J. Atkinson; front: D. Collister, H. Henney, A. Walker, P. Charlton, A. Banks, D. McMillan, H. Marland, I. MacCorquodale.
(Courtesy *Rugby League Journal*)

Workington Town on a cold Cumbria day. (Courtesy *Rugby League Journal*)

7. A year in Cumbria: Workington Town

Jim had been playing under a cloud since the John Greengrass incident. He found he was waiting for the referee's whistle every time he made a tackle. His form didn't drop as he was still making those crunching runs in midfield but he thought that if he was dismissed again so soon after this battle with the RFL, they would take him to the cleaners.

Jim received a phone call from Tom Mitchell, the chairman at Workington Town. "Listen Jim" said Tom Mitchell, "I have had a word with Vincent [Karalius] and I have put a proposition to him that we sign you at Workington to take you out of the limelight of that First Division for a season or so. Come up to Derwent Park and I will look after you. For our part we need a big front rower and if we get you I am sure we will get promotion into the First Division. Stay with us to cement a place for another season then I will let you go back to Widnes on a return transfer." Jim thought for a moment then replied: "Tom, it's a hell of a way up and down to Workington and on training nights I would have to take time off my new job, so it's a nonstarter." The shrewd Mitchell responded 'I have already sorted out your training; you will do it with Vincent! I only want you up to Workington on playing days. Your job will be safe, Vincent will see to your fitness and I will see to it that there is no further nonsense with referees.' I thought what is there to lose! So I agreed, so long as everything was all right with Vince and Widnes."

So, on the evening of 5 February 1976, just before the Challenge Cup deadline, Jim joined Workington Town for a fee of £6,250. Just a week after the Player's No.6 Trophy final with Widnes, Jim made his debut for Workington Town at Thrum Hall against Halifax in the Second Division.

Workington Town joined the RFL in 1945, finally bringing a professional presence to the game in Cumberland. They won the Championship in 1951 and the Challenge Cup in 1952, led by Gus Risman. There were two more Challenge Cup Final appearances in the 1950s, but they struggled in the 1960s and when the league split into two divisions in 1973, were in the lower tier. But the team that Jim was joining had some quality players, including full-back Paul Charlton, John Risman and Iain MacCorquodale on the wings, scrum-half Arnie Walker and the Gorley brothers, Peter and Les, and Eddie Bowman in the pack.

Tom Mitchell was for many years the driving force behind Workington Town RLFC. In 1998, he published his autobiography – *The Memoirs and Sporting Life of Tom Mitchell*. He had a remarkably full life, including being one of the managers on the controversial 1958 Lions tour. One of the chapters covers different players he knew and admired over the years – most, understandably with a link to Workington Town. The piece on James ('BIG JIM') Mills gives an insight into how he signed Jim for Workington and the respect he had for Jim.

He had read in the newspapers that Salford were looking to bring Jim back to The Willows. He was shocked, and recalled: "Salford for a long time had garnered the reputation of being the game's cleanest exponent of the art of rugby at its best. Their forwards were efficient but 'gentlemanly'. They had a brilliant back division of several top class union converts. The name of Mills should have meant anathema to their style but I strongly suspect that chairman Brain Snape (ex R.U. with Waterloo) finally decided that just being nice guys was not on any longer.

But Mills of all people? A towering figure of a man whose visage off the field was serene, but on it most menacing. He had been coast as a 'Villain' after one or two of his excursions into questionable behaviour, especially on the International scene. That is putting it euphemistically, my friends will insist."

Mitchell outlined that at this particular meeting of the Rugby League Council he made sure he sat next to Harry Ditchfield, the Widnes representative on the Council. Snape was chairing the meeting, and Mitchell enquired if the deal with Salford was concluded, and what the fee was. He also took advantage of his friendship with Vince Karalius. He recalled: "Just outside the Council Chamber I phoned Bill Whalley, Secretary of 'Town' and asked him to get himself down to Widnes pronto with director Jack Atkinson and a cheque. I had ensured that Jim Mills was taken out of circulation and secreted in the Karalius home – a hijacking if you like – but it was necessary – very!" Snape had beaten Mitchell to the signing of England rugby union winger Keith Fielding, so Mitchell was happy to pip Salford to the post for Jim's signature.

Mitchell commented that Jim made an immediate impact at Workington: "...all the forwards respected him for a start, having tangled with him as an opponent. At this stage in his career his very presence was unnerving to those who crossed his path."

Understandably, Mitchell was concerned about Jim's disciplinary record. In a crucial promotion match at Bramley, the last match of the season, he urged Jim to stay on the pitch for 80 minutes. Two points for Workington could clinch promotion. In the first half Mitchell says that "...a fierce looking Bramley forward... shot past me in full flight on the wing of all places ... in his path James Mills Esq. So I looked away and shuddered. Touch judge and referee consulting, with the prostate player in full view." But fortunately only a penalty was given. In the dressing room at half-time, Mitchell said "Jim, you were as near as dammit sent off in spite of what you were told as you went out." Jim replied: "Before you go on, Tom, I had nothing to do with it; I can't help it if somebody runs straight into me – do you expect me to stand aside? Anyway, I got the right fellow – he had gone berserk."

In the *Rugby Leaguer*, Alan Irving, who covered Workington and Whitehaven for the paper, was delighted at the club's new acquisition. On 25 February he wrote: "Is the sensational signing of mighty Jim Mills from Widnes the last, vital piece to complete the Workington Town jigsaw? There is an old saying in rugby league that a team can have the best backs in the world but still win nothing if the forwards are not good enough. This has certainly been the case at Workington. Although their backs have been and still are First Division class, Town have continued to languish in Division Two and been knocked out of sudden-death competitions at the vital stage because there had been something missing up front. Now that missing link has been found in the formidable shape of 6ft 2 17-stone Jim Mills.

He is the powerful, classy, ball-playing packman the Cumbrians have sought since Brian Edgar's retirement. Like ex-Great Britain skipper Edgar, Mills is devastating on the break. And the prospect of Big Jim using his power to set up openings for spectacular runners like Eddie Bowman and Les Gorley is also exciting.

If Town don't make the First Division after this super signing it will be nothing short of a tragedy, especially as lower-grade rugby is hardly likely to be the liking of one of the world's great forwards. The Cumbrians' enterprise deserves the kind of success that has eluded them since the 1950s when they went to Wembley three times. Will Mills help bring back glories as well as many of the Town's lost legions? And how long will the 29-year-old Welsh giant stay at Derwent Park?"

Jim trained with Vince Karalius in Widnes, and travelled up to Workington on Thursdays, and for home matches. He often linked up with Lancashire based Iain MacCorquodale for the journey up north.

Jim played in Workington's final 10 matches of the 1975–76 season. Only one was lost, at Keighley in the second round of the Challenge Cup. But the key aim was promotion, which was secured on the last day of the season. Jim scored three tries, including two in a 44–8 win at Tattersfield against perennial strugglers Doncaster.

Looking forward to life in the First Division, Alan Irving wrote: "...in Charlton and Big Jim Mills, Town have two big-time players whose experience should help a young team achieve the level of consistency needed against top-class opposition week in, week out."

The Cumberland-based clubs had always entered the Lancashire Cup. However, neither Whitehaven or Workington Town had ever reached the final – Barrow were seen as a Lancashire club in those days. The previous season Workington had been beaten by Jim's Widnes team in the final. In 1976–77, the first two rounds were played in the first two weeks of the season. Jim played in both matches; a narrow win over Swinton, and more comfortable one over Blackpool. The season had barely started and Workington were in a cup semi-final. But the draw produced a tough trip to Wilderspool to face Warrington. On 12 September Workington had played there in the league, lost 16–9 and Jim had been sent off for a 'vicious late head tackle'. However, his three match ban for this latest indiscretion did not start until the beginning of October, so he could play in the semi-final. Workington got a 9–9 draw at Wilderspool on 21 September, and eight days later, Warrington travelled up the M6 to Derwent Park for the replay. Joe Holliday, in his club history, writes that "Town, and in particular Jim Mills, were magnificent as they threw the ball about with six players scoring a try each plus four goals for Iain MacCorquodale, amassing 26 points to Warrington's 15."

Fortunately, Jim had served his suspension by 30 October, when, inevitably, Workington faced Widnes in the final. In his preview in the *Leaguer*, Don Yates wrote: "The Workington pack, which includes former Widnes hard-man Jim Mills, is reputed to be the strongest in the game..." The result was close, Widnes won 16–11, after being 9–5 ahead at the break. But they only scored one try, from centre Ray Wilkins; the rest of their points came from MacCorquodale's boot.

Left: Little and large! Great Britain team-mates Roger Millward and Jim during Jim's time at Workington.

Middle: Jim with Vince Karalius and Tom Mitchell on the Isle of Man.

Bottom: The teams from the 1976 Lancashire Cup semi-final reply between Workington and Warrington.

FORSHAWS LANCASHIRE CUP							SEMI-FINAL REPLAY
WORKINGTON TOWN	T	G	DG	T	G	DG	**WARRINGTON**
							DEREK FINNEGAN 1
1 PAUL CHARLTON (Capt.)							DAVID SUTTON 2
2 DAVID COLLISTER							DAVID CUNLIFFE 3
3 RAY WILKINS							RON CLARK 4
4 IAN WRIGHT							DEREK WHITEHEAD 5
5 IAIN MacCORQUODALE							GLEN KNIGHT 6
6 BRIAN LAUDER							HARRY GORDON 7
7 ARNOLD WALKER							BRIAN BUTLER 8
8 JIM MILLS							TONY MILLER 9
9 ALAN BANKS							JOE PRICE 10
10 RALPH CALVIN							TOMMY MARTYN 11
11 LES GORLEY							MIKE NICHOLAS 12
12 EDDIE BOWMAN							BARRY PHILBIN 13
13 PETER GORLEY							14
14 BILL PATTINSON							BOB WONBORN 15
15							
							Touch Judges :
Referee : Mr. W. H. Thompson							Mr. J. H. Ross
Timekeeper : A. Murray							Mr. T. Dawes

Jim recalls: "I felt for the Workington board and in particular Tom Mitchell. One incident happened when in front of the main stand, Mick Adams tackled me and for a bit of fun I rubbed my forehead across his nose pretending to head-butt him. We had a laugh, but I didn't know that Mick's sister and her husband, who both followed Widnes, were sitting in front of us. It looked as though I had stuck the nut on Mick and I could hear her as she blasted me for using the nut on her brother. After the game we were having a beer and Mick invited me to go to his sister's party at their house. Mick and I arrived; he rang the doorbell and darted around the corner leaving me there on my own. Through the glass in the door I made out Mick's sister coming and I heard her say, 'It had better not be that dirty Jim Mills'. When she saw me stood there on my own she took a deep breath and smiling said 'Come in Jim and join the party!' Mick had set me up good and proper and he was helpless with laughter when he came in minutes later.

Little things like that and seeing the comradeship of the players at the party made me realise that it was time I came back to reality. I had been out of the way long enough and much as I loved playing at Workington I suppose I had become a Widnes lad at heart. So I decided to see Tom Mitchell and ask him to let me return to Lancashire to be nearer home."

There was one more controversial incident before Jim returned to Widnes. Playing at Odsal on 30 November, Jim recalls "There was a bit of nonsense going on with an odd punch or two but the incident was absolutely nothing. I had taken a tackle and the Bradford player was lying on one of my legs, As he rolled away I lifted my leg over him to regain my feet when suddenly he did a 'dying swan' act and played dead. As the referee sent me off I glanced at him and he was winking to his mates and smiling. I received a three match ban."

Jim's final game for Workington Town was on 9 January. He recalls: "I had become fed up with all the travelling and had asked Tom Mitchell for a move to Lancashire. I was still training with Vinny Karalius each day and now he was coaching at Wigan He told me that he would take me on at Wigan anytime as a player, but it depended on how much Workington would let me go for. It was put in the newspaper that Workington wanted £8,000 for me but I told the reporters, 'Who is going to pay £8,000 for a 31-year-old prop with a disciplinary record like mine?"

Both St Helens and Wigan made bids for Jim, but both were below Workington's price. Jim was so fed up that he "decided to retire from the game. Straight away I received an offer to become a wrestler. I fancied it too, the promoter even had a name picked out for me and I went along to Warrington to see a couple of bouts. My new name would be 'Gentleman Jim' but again I decided 'no'. For once I made the correct decision because I had a phone call from the Welsh coach; my old mate David Watkins, asking how I was keeping. He enquired about my fitness, which was OK because I had only recently called it a day. He asked me to play for Wales against England on 29 January at Leeds, which I did." Wales won 6–2, and Jim was still on Workington's books at the time. But soon a deal was agreed with Widnes, and Jim returned to action for the Chemics on 6 February 1977 at Wakefield.

Tom Mitchell had hoped Jim would stay with Workington for three years. He recalled in his autobiography a version of events, that shows the club in a better light: "There was, however, a gentleman's agreement that, if ever, for any good reason he wished to leave I would not stand in his way. His request, when it came, was entirely unexpected. I visited the Welsh dressing room at Headingley... before an international match. He asked if he could have a word with me. His business career was shaping up to the point where he really could not make three visits to Workington every other week ... 'I'm no good for you now Tom, just let me get away – it's been great playing for Town and I became good friends with the rest of the pack.'

Mitchell also recalls that the only 'back hander' Jim got from the club was a made to measure blazer for a key Lancashire Cup match. He says "Trousers were added to make up a suit – the first one he had ever worn – nothing off the peg ever fitted Jim." He also comments that Jim was "a fine club man with a great sense of fun," and said that when Jim left the club "I missed him!"

Workington finished in 12th place in the league, just above the relegation places. But the four-up, four-down system meant that the promoted teams often struggled. To consolidate a First Division place was itself an achievement. Jim played in 13 matches for Workington in his second season at the club, and had contributed to First Division survival, and a first Lancashire Cup Final. Ironically for Jim, Workington built on their experience in the Lancashire Cup to win it in 1977–78, knocking out Widnes in the second round on their way to the final.

A cold day in 1978.

8. The Cup Kings: Widnes 1977 to 1980

So, on 4 February 1977 Jim rejoined Widnes. In his time in Cumbria the Chemics had continued to enhance their reputation as the 'Cup Kings' and reached the 1976 Challenge Cup Final, but had lost 20–5 to St Helens. They had also won the Lancashire Cup against Jim's Workington Town. Frank Myler was still the Widnes coach.

The next three years saw Jim involved in eight finals, including another two Wembley appearances, and win the First Division Championship. The latter was particularly significant because it was the first time that Widnes won a league title.

Jim's second match back at Widnes was at Bramley in the Challenge Cup. He scored a try – Widnes's other touchdown came from fellow prop Bill Ramsey – and followed this with two against Swinton in the second round. Further wins against Bradford Northern and Hull KR took Widnes back to Wembley against Leeds.

Widnes were making their third consecutive Challenge Cup Final appearance, equalling Bradford Northern's record in the 1940s, and were favourites. However, both teams had finished in mid-table in the league, Leeds were ninth and Widnes 10th, both on 30 points.

After the teams had exchanged early penalty goals, Widnes took the lead through a converted Mal Aspey try. Atkinson pulled one back for Leeds, but the Chemics were 7–5 up at the break. But on 53 minutes a Les Dyl try put Leeds ahead and they never looked back, winning 16–7.

Jim recalls that "I had injured my shoulder just before the Wembley match. Tony Gourley had kneed me in the shoulder when I was on the ground after a tackle and damaged it. I was upset because I knew that Wembley wasn't far away. In the next scrum I punched Gourley, which resulted in Kel Coslett the Rochdale player-coach taking Gourley off. At the end of the game near the tunnel at Naughton Park, Gourley approached me to shake hands and I punched him again. The Rochdale chairman, Jack Grindrod witnessed the incident, and said that he was going to have me reported and banned for punching Gourley in the tunnel. He told Kel Coslett, the Rochdale player-coach, and Kel tried to cool him down and to forget about it, but Jack Grindrod insisted an apology was in order. Unknown to me, Kel asked our captain, Doug Laughton, to apologise on my behalf, because there was no point in asking me. I did not find this out until a few weeks later that Doug had apologised, which may have resulted in me missing out on Wembley had I received a ban.

I had treatment for my shoulder and went to see a specialist. He gave my cortisone injections, but I had damaged the ligaments. I asked him if I could play at Wembley. 'Only you can tell', he replied. I hoped it would be okay. We were red hot favourites because we had beaten them convincingly at Headingley earlier in the season. Frank Myler had people running at me in training to test the injury. It was the only game in which I ever wore shoulder pads. But in the first five minutes I made a tackle, my arm was left hanging down, and I was largely a passenger for the rest of the game."

Jim recalls that nothing went right for Widnes: "They kicked for the corner and the ball bounced back and John Atkinson scored. Then we won the ball from a scrum, but Reg Bowden's pass hit the referee. We had to scrum down again; they got the ball and scored. I learnt a lesson that day – never play if you're not right with an injury." Widnes had been 7–5 ahead, but, as Jim acknowledges, runs by Steve Pitchford, who won the Lance Todd Trophy, caused Widnes problems. Once Leeds took the lead they Widnes could not come back into the game and the Yorkshire side went on to win 16–7.

Around 20,000 supporters had followed Widnes to Wembley, and many turned out to welcome the team home. But more success was just around the corner. Jim had played in 14 matches since his return to the club, had scored four tries and did not have any disciplinary problems.

1977–78

Widnes had clearly established their credentials as a cup side, but it can be argued that the best test of a great team is the league championship. To win the title, consistency is the key, and Widnes were truly magnificent in the 1977–78 league championship race.

A second round exit in the Lancashire Cup – to Workington Town – was followed by a narrow defeat at Wigan in the team's second league match. But 12 successive victories followed until St Helens beat the Chemics 16–3 at Knowsley Road on New Year's Eve. But after that, only two more league matches were lost, at Featherstone and Leeds, and the title was won by five points. Widnes won every league match at Naughton Park, and finished with a points scored difference of 372, scoring 613 and conceding 241.

Often teams that win the league make little progress in the cups, but Widnes also reached two finals. In the John Player Trophy they went down narrowly to Warrington, 9–4, and in the end-of-season Premiership, lost 17–8 to Bradford Northern in the final. Jim missed the match against Warrington through suspension, but played in the Premiership Final against Bradford Northern. Jim says that Widnes would have beaten Northern had it not been for the state of the pitch: "Once again we were hot favourites to win this game, but there had been heavy rain that week and Wilderspool were the final was being played was a mudbath, and this did not suit the Widnes type of play, had it been a fine day I'm sure we would have beaten them."

Jim recalls that Kenny Gill was signed from Salford during the season, and slotted in at stand-off. This allowed David Eckersley to move to full-back, and Eric Hughes to play at centre.

Jim played 29 matches, and scored six tries. He injured his foot playing against Leeds in the BBC2 Floodlit Trophy on 27 September, and missed seven matches. On the disciplinary front, he was given a one match suspension for two cautions at the end of December, and was sent off twice. Once was against Wigan on 11 January 1978, for punching Wigan's Bill Ashurst, for which he got a two match ban. Wigan's coach was Vince Karalius, and he had told Ashurst to 'wind up' Jim, hoping to provoke a reaction. That part of the plan was successful, but Ashurst being carried off probably was not. Brian Batty's report in the *Daily Mail* said that in the eighth minute "There was a violent clash of heads as Mills roared in and punches appeared to be flung before Pudsey referee Joe Jackson waved Mills to the dressing room." However, in Jim's defence, Batty reports Widnes chairman Jack Woodward saying: "We are not making excuses, but we are bitterly upset at the dismissal of Mills, for he was severely provoked. It was a case of the man who retaliates getting sent off, but he had been struck first in an earlier incident and suffered for it."

Jim was also sent off, again for punching, on 26 February against Rochdale Hornets and was given a one match ban. At the end of the season, Frank Myler retired as coach and was replaced by Doug Laughton, who became player-coach, and coached the team for the rest of Jim's time as a player at the club.

Jim passing to Mick Adams against Hull KR in the 1977 Cup semi-final.

Doug Laughton on the attack in the 1977 Challenge Cup Final. Doug was
a team-mate of Jim's during his time at Widnes and is a close friend.
(Photo: Aaron Photography)

A report at the end of the season said that Widnes were considering offering Jim a coaching role along with Laughton. The report by Brian Batty in the *Daily Mail* quoted Jim as saying "I have always fancied the coaching side of the game and since Doug Laughton had a talk with me about helping him out next season I shall think it over."

Interviewed for this book, Jim outlined that "I was assistant coach to Doug Laughton for a season towards the end of my playing career. Doug asked me to help out, and I got a bit of extra money from the club for it. He had a business, and I took training if he couldn't make it. When I retired I got involved in my nightclub business, so the question of coaching never came up. I wouldn't have been a great coach; I was too friendly with the players."

Later on, his son David took up the game, but Jim, while being supportive, stood back: "With David, I didn't get involved. I never asked him to play. John Hodgson, who was not a board member at that time, had a son, Richard, who played for St Maries juniors in Widnes. John asked David if he would like to join the team and give it a go to see if he liked it. That's where it all started for David; he went on to join St Helens Crusaders, and was selected to go on the North West Counties Juniors tour of Australia and New Zealand and Fiji, which was a wonderful experience for him. George Nicholls was on the management team of the tour. After the tour, one of the Widnes scouts recommended that Dougie watch David, and Dougie decided to sign David on at Widnes.

I used to go to the matches sometimes. But I found that some of the parents were over the top, expecting too much and screaming from the touchline. Ruth always used to go the matches. I remember once, she came home and David's team had been playing Waterhead, from Oldham. She said to me that there was a 12-year-old called Kevin Sinfield playing for them, who she thought was 'going to be a smashing player' and that we should sign him. I said to her 'just watch the games, we'll choose the players.' She still reminds me about it.

With young players you see some talented players, but they don't always make it. Sometimes they go off in a different direction, it depends how seriously they take it." However, it is interesting to speculate about how Widnes might have fared had Jim listened to Ruth...

Jim had considered retiring at the end of the previous season, but in fact had almost two seasons and another international tour before hanging up his boots. Despite being aged 34, he had a very productive season, scoring 13 tries, an incredible figure for a prop forward, and making 34 appearances. It would have been more, but for two four-match suspensions, both for being sent off against Warrington.

Local derbies against Warrington were fiercely contested. Fellow Welshman Mike Nicholas was one of the key members of the Warrington pack, and, like Jim, could look after himself if things got tough. The well-known referee, Billy Thompson, recalls one match at Wilderspool: "The two teams were waiting to go onto the pitch. Mike said to Jim: 'How are you doing?' Jim replied: 'How am I doing? I'm going to give you plenty of this [waving his fist] and kick you between the posts.' Mike said to me: 'Billy, are you listening to this?' I replied: 'He's not talking to me…'" In fact, it was Billy who sent Jim off against Warrington in January.

Mike Nicholas was often involved in battles with Jim in the local derbies with Warrington. Interviewed for this book, he outlined: "Jim is a little older than me. I started in the Aberavon first team in 1965, so I never played against him in rugby union. I signed for Warrington in 1972, and I think Jim was at his best when he played for Widnes. Vince Karalius put a lot of emphasis on fitness, and Jim was then at his best 'fighting' weight of 17 and a half stone. He was at his most effective then – he was big and had a physical presence. Some big guys didn't need to intimidate people, but Jim had both – he was a formidable player, but could also be difficult to play against. It made things interesting. He was always prepared to confront the tough guys from other teams.

He became the 'enforcer' for Widnes, and I had the same role for Warrington, so there were clashes. But the game was different then. There was an acceptable ingredient of violence; it wasn't policed as it is now. Jim was the talisman for Widnes, and it was almost like pantomime villains – people came to the matches expecting a clash between us. The state of the game when we played gave you a lot of licence, which created alter egos (dark side) players who got dragged down to a pretty primitive level in order to survive the gladiatorial skulduggery demanded in what had become a rugby league amphitheatre. In other words Jim and I had become a product of a game plumbing the depths of its physicality. Well, that's our excuse anyway.

Looking back, I think things needed to change in the game as far as discipline was concerned. It had lost its 'charm'. Some of the local derbies – I was sent off in one; Widnes had three players sent off, and Alex Murphy was so angry he had to be restrained in the tunnel by the police chief superintendent at half-time. I remember Jim trying to mediate in that game!

Jim was most effective when he was coming through with the ball. I remember in the 1979 John Player Final, people were hanging off him trying to stop him. Jim got sent off for hitting me, but I should never have played – I'd broken my jaw against Bradford in the Premiership semi-final just before the match.

Another time, when he was playing for Workington, he was coming through us all the time. I flew at him, and he got a cut. It was like waking a sleeping giant. He didn't get hold of me, but two of our players did go off injured. The others were telling me to leave him alone!

A few days after that incident, we were training with Wales at Swinton. Jim was still sporting the battle scars I had been responsible for. The players were aghast at the damage he'd received and were enquiring about the whereabouts and time of the funeral of the person who had the temerity to take such a liberty. Ronnie Simpson, the Welsh manager, was going round asking for everyone's measurements. Jim gave him his, and then asked for mine. Ronnie asked why? 'For his coffin' was the answer – 'Next time you're dead' he said to me. Everyone cringed.

But usually Jim was nice off the pitch; a tremendous guy. But on it he was the hardest, toughest guy I played against."

Widnes could not retain the league title, although they came close, finishing third, just two points behind champions Hull KR. But in the cups, it was a magnificent season. In the Lancashire Cup, Widnes faced Workington Town in the final at Central Park, and won 15–13 after being 11–5 down at half-time. Two months later, Widnes travelled to Knowsley Road to face St Helens in the BBC2 Floodlit Trophy Final, and won 13–7. Next came the John Player Trophy; and another trip to Knowsley Road, this time to face Warrington on 28 April. The scores were level at half-time, 2–2, but Widnes ran away with the match in the second half to win 28–4, despite Jim being sent off by Fred Lindop for punching. He was given a four match ban, but this was not imposed until he was on the Lions tour, so he did not miss out on Wembley the following week. It was his final sending off in rugby league. Jim says that "I was sent off in this match for punching Mike Nicholas late on in the game when the game was won. I think that Mike should have been sent off for refusing to fight, which I still tell him today; he is a good friend, and we have a laugh over it."

In the Challenge Cup, Widnes beat Workington Town and Wigan at Naughton Park before winning 14–0 at Huddersfield in the third round. In the semi-final they narrowly beat Bradford Northern 14–11 at Station Road to set up a Wembley final against Wakefield Trinity.

It was Trinity's first final appearance since the notorious 1968 'watersplash' final. It was Jim's final appearance as a player at Wembley, and he recalls: "It wasn't a great spectacle, really a scrappy match. We didn't play particularly well, but won it. The Lance Todd Trophy went to David Topliss, who played well. We won with a couple of tries, and they scored late on."

The first half was scoreless. A Mick Burke penalty put Widnes ahead, then Stuart Wright kicked for the corner and scored. Mick Burke's touchline conversion put Widnes 7–0 ahead, a drop-goal from Keith Elwell made it 8–0. Wakefield replied with a score by Andy Fletcher, but a try from Eric Hughes and drop-goal from David Eckersley made the final score 12–3. It was Jim's last rugby league final as a player.

During the season, there was a surprise possibility of Jim moving to France. Suspended after being sent off against Warrington, he went to watch Wales play France in Narbonne in February.

Press reports said that Jim was offered £7,000 to play for St Jacques in the 1979–80 season, as well as a flat and a job. Mick Murphy was the club's player-coach, but wanted to return home and saw Jim as a possible replacement. Jim was reported as saying that he would discuss the offer with Jack Woodward when he came home from his trip with Wales. However, nothing came of the potential move, and Jim stayed at Widnes for one more season.

The 1978 Widnes team with the Championship trophy: Ken Gill, Reg Bowden, Mal Aspey, Bill Ramsey, Doug Laughton, Keith Elwell, Jim, David Hull, Stuart Wright, Eric Hughes, Paul Woods, Glyn Shaw, mascot Paul Hansbury.

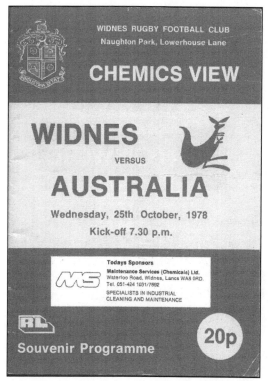

The last club team to beat the Kangaroos.

Top: In action for Widnes
against Warrington in the 1979
John Player Trophy Final.
Left: Ready for the kick-off.

Left: Reg Bowden with the Division One Trophy in 1978. Reg played with Jim during all Jim's career with Widnes.

Below: Jim and Glyn Shaw celebrate the 1979 Challenge Cup Final win at Wembley.

(Both photos: Aaron Photography)

1979–80

Jim's final season as a player saw him play 16 times, although five of those were off the bench. He scored two tries. He had come home early from the Lions tour of Australia, and didn't make his first appearance for Widnes until the end of September. He missed out on a victory in the Lancashire Cup Final, against Workington, and a defeat to Bradford Northern in the John Player Trophy final on 5 January at Headingley. Widnes got their revenge on the team that had beaten them to the title by one point in the Premiership final at Station Road on 17 May, winning 19–5. But by then Jim had retired.

Jim's best run of appearances this season came in March, with five consecutive starts. But an injury against Bradford Northern at Widnes on 19 March forced him into retirement. He remembers it well: "I'd had a bad knee injury for years, since the 1974 tour. It got worse and worse. I came home early from the 1979 tour; the hard grounds in Australia had made my knee swell up.

We played Bradford Northern at Widnes. There was a loose ball, I kicked at it, and David Redfearn dived across and his body hit my knee. The ligaments snapped and broke away from the bone. I never played again. I had an operation, and the surgeon said that if I was younger I could have made a comeback, but I'd done everything in the game, so I decided to call it a day."

Frank Myler coached Jim at Widnes after Vince Karalius left the club, and worked with him when Jim was club chairman. Frank knows him well, and they are close friends: "As a player, Jim was a big man, could run a bit, and was very aggressive. I would have him in my team any time. Jim had speed, and was a good player. He scored at Wembley in 1975. He was 19 stone in those days, which was a lot to carry around. He would have been a good player in any era, and could have played today. Whatever club he was playing for, he always performed."

As his coach, Myler says that Jim "Was very keen as a player, and was also very funny. He could lighten the mood with the players, and was well liked." He also tried to deal with Jim's disciplinary problems: "He could play, and he never bothered with anyone, but anyone who tried it on with him must have been very brave. He always reacted, which wasn't the best. He had a little bit of a temper. I tried to change him, to talk to him, and he would be sincere, and say he would behave himself, but if someone gave him one, he would always give one back. But he was a gentle fellow off the field. He was one of the all-time greats at Widnes, and brought spirit to the club. But he fell for people winding him up, he was a better player than people realised, and a player to have in your side. He wouldn't hesitate to retaliate, and he suffered through it with suspensions and missing matches."

Reg Bowden played at scrum-half for Widnes for the whole of Jim's time with the club. He believes that Jim was a very important member of the Widnes of the 1970s: "As a player, Jim was one of the best prop forwards. He was aggressive, fast and strong, and could do 100 yards in 12 seconds. He was someone you wanted on your side – if anything happened in a game you could stay behind him, which I used to do.

I remember when Jim came back from Australia. There were five of us with him, all smaller members of the team, with this giant. He was 20 stone, ginormous, but what a player he turned out to be. I said to him 'I hope you're not as daft as you're big' and he picked me up with one hand. He was outstanding in the 1975 Challenge Cup Final against Warrington. Another great match was against the Australian tourists in 1978, when we beat them. They were so upset that they didn't come in the clubhouse afterwards.

We also had some big matches with Bradford Northern. Jim was magnificent in those sort of games [Bradford had a huge pack], he was a deterrent as soon as he walked onto the pitch. He was a hard forward, but also a great rugby league player. He was different from players such as Bill Ramsey and Ian van Bellen, because on the pitch he had a nasty streak. He was a big man, and there was only one Jim Mills. He was a nice man off the pitch, but on the pitch sometimes the 'blue mist' came and he would want to win at all costs. Opposing players 'stayed tackled' and sometimes Jim would give someone a clout – it was all about winning. He would not allow his team-mates to go backwards. He never believed we would be beaten. He brought the best out of the Widnes players, and was a major reason for our success. We missed him when he was at Workington, and Keith Elwell and I went to Frank Myler to say that we had to get him back. We were being intimidated without him, whereas normally we intimidated the other team. No one ever got the better of Jim. Once it was raised that his tackle count was low. Jim pointed out that players would run at me or Keith Elwell rather than him. Stats don't always tell the whole story.

But off the field he was one of the nicest people you could meet. Nothing was too much trouble for him, and he was very placid off the pitch. He is always good company; we go out, reminisce about the old times, and he sings as well. He could laugh at himself as well. He used to tell a story about how he'd been sent off at Leigh early in the game, got changed and gone home. He lived near the Widnes ground at the time, and as he was walking home, asked someone how Widnes had got on. 'They won, but Mills got sent off, the prat,' was the reply. He is one of the gentlemen of the game; we won't see another like Big Jim."

At Widnes Jim played with some of the club's greatest players. They were mainly a local team, unlike the next generation which had major Welsh and international signings. Looking back he reflects on some of his team-mates from his time at Naughton Park: "Playing with Reg Bowden was like having another forward in the team. He was so strong. Once he stopped Ian van Bellen [a 6 feet tall, 18 stone prop] in his tracks. He was always upsetting the other side with his talking during matches. He did a lot of 'sweeping' behind our line of defence. We used man-to-man marking then, rather than sliding across like today. If someone broke through, he would cover us. He was a good tackler, and a good footballer. He never got capped, but there were a lot of good scrum-halves then.

Doug Laughton was a great forward, and added experience to the team when he joined us. He had a great turn of speed, and for me was great to run off. He could weigh the game up, and would run wide, spot gaps, and pass or go through himself. When I was in Australia in 1970, I watched the third test, and he was the man-of-the-match. He had a marvellous game that day. He did a grand job for Widnes.

Mick Adams was another good passer, who I could run off. He was a great tackler, and good kicker of the ball. He would aim for the crossbar or the uprights, and we would follow up the kicks and score. He was a good all-round forward.

Keith Elwell holds the record for consecutive appearances for one club [239 for Widnes from 1977 to 1982]. One week, he split his head open and we thought he would miss a game. But he played the next week, with his head wrapped in bandages. He wasn't big, but he was a tough lad, quick, and a good drop-goal kicker. Hooker was a crucial position in those days, and we had some good props to play with him.

Bill Ramsey was a good prop, with great experience in the game. Another one was Glyn Shaw, who came to us from Welsh rugby union in 1977. He still lives in Widnes. He was a Welsh international, and gave good service to the club. He was a very fit and strong forward, and played in the 1979 Challenge Cup Final.

Another Welsh player was Paul Woods, who was scrum-half or full-back and was very tough and uncompromising. I remember him playing for Wales against Australia. He had Tommy Raudonikis complaining to the referee all the time. Sadly he died of Leukaemia in November 2007.

Brian Hogan was a good strong forward, who had great experience. Barry Sheridan was another quality forward who played well at Wembley in 1975. Bob Blackwood, a Cumbrian, was as tough as they come. When we played the Australian touring side at Widnes, John O'Neill the big Australian prop, clashed with Bob and ended up with a broken jaw, which resulted in him going home from the tour. Bob is a great friend of mine. David Hull was a very good forward who we signed from St Helens, and gave the club great service. Alan Dearden was one of the best tacklers I've ever seen; he used to tackle them round the ankles with devastating force, a great forward. John Wood and Mike O'Neill were both young forwards with potential, and Mike gave long service to the club.

At full-back, Ray Dutton was a very good player. He was steady, dependable a good defender and goalkicker as well. Later on, Mick Burke took over at full-back. Doug Laughton signed him. He was another great goalkicker; like Terry Price; he was very relaxed when he kicked. He won the Lancashire Cup for us with a touchline conversion.

On the wing, Stuart Wright was a great player, who scored a lot of tries. He was very fast, and a good finisher. He could make a try out of nothing, often by kicking forward. For a couple of seasons we had Chris Anderson on the wing. He was an Australian international, and later was player-coach at Halifax and coached Australia. I remember in one of the test matches in 1978, I got Graham Olling, and Chris complained to the referee, trying to get me sent off. I told Chris he was a 'tell-tale'! Alan Prescott played in the Challenge Cup Final against Workington. He was quite short, but very strong. Another winger was Dennis Brown, who played with me in the Cardiff Schoolboys, and went on to be a Royal Marine, and travelled from Plymouth to play. He was a good, strong wingman.

At centre, Eric Hughes had tremendous pace. He would be on my shoulder if I made a break to back me up. He was another tremendous finisher. He was tough in his own way, and very fast. Mal Aspey was another very good centre, who had a long career in the game. Mick George, was a strong running centre, he was also a great comic in the dressing room."

Tommy Warburton was a good player who could slot into any position in the backs as could Dave Eckersley, another fine player. Dennis and Jimmy O'Neill were two brothers who gave great service to Widnes. Dennis had tremendous pace, and was tipped to get to the very top until a bad injury set him back."

Photo: Jim and a young Bobbie Goulding in 1979, with Widnes's cups. Bobbie went on to have a very successful rugby league career.

9. A British Lion

Jim played six test matches for Great Britain, a combination of injury – missing the 1977 World Cup and his knee injury on the 1979 tour – and not going on the 1970 tour restricting his opportunities for the game's highest international honour. However, he was on the winning side in three of his six appearances. All his appearances were against Australia or New Zealand.

As Jim proudly points out: "In 1970s, I was selected for every tour: 1970, 1974, 1975 for Wales, 1977, 1979. I was the only forward to be chosen for all of them. Roger Millward was as well, although for England in 1975."

Jim's first international tour was to Australia and New Zealand in 1974. He was in familiar company, with six of the tourists being Welsh, including Maurice Richards who joined the tour on 6 July to cover for injured players. The others were Colin Dixon, Dave Willicombe, John Bevan and David Watkins. Dixon and Richards had played union with Jim at Cardiff, while David Watkins was playing for Newport at that time. Jim recalls that "It was a good side. Chris Hesketh was the captain, and George Nicholls, who had played with me at Widnes, was one of the key forwards. Jim Challinor was a good coach. The tour manager was Reg Parker. He did a great job, and all the players liked him. He had played for Barrow and was chairman of Blackpool."

The Lions had won the series in Australia in 1970, when Jim was playing for North Sydney, but in 1973, the Australians had won 2–1 in Great Britain. The Lions had won the first test, but then the Australians had come back to win the series. Robert Gate described the tackling in the second test as "almost suicidal" and said that the game "was not for the faint hearted." The Lions knew what to expect, but also faced playing on hard pitches, and with Australian referees. Jim says that "With their referees we had to be a lot better than them to beat them."

Another problem for the Lions was an extremely demanding schedule, with tough midweek matches often scheduled before test matches. The Lions played their first match in Australia in Darwin on 26 May. Their last game was almost two months later, on 21 July. In less than two months they played 21 matches. This included two weeks where they played on Tuesday and Thursday, and four weekends when they fielded teams on a Saturday and Sunday.

The 1974 Great Britain squad (Courtesy *Rugby League Journal*)

The tour started in Darwin, then moved into Queensland, and finished in New South Wales. Jim recalls that "The matches against Queensland and New South Wales were like test matches, and we played them the week before a test match. And in the country games, all the players were waiting to get stuck into you, to make their names playing against Great Britain. It was a very hard tour. We had our own plane, and the hotels and motels were ok."

The Lions used 29 players on tour, although this included Jim Challinor, who played a game in New Zealand. Jim made his test debut in the first test, which the Lions lost 12–6. It was generally described as a dull game, witnessed by Australian Prime Minister Gough Whitlam. There was only one try, but with the score 11–4 with 19 minutes left, Steve Nash was tackled as he went to touch down by the posts. Jim says that "I would not blame Steve. He took a hard tackle as he went over the try line. It was late on in the game and would have won us the test."

The Lions were badly hit by injuries, and for the first time flew out two extra players. Four test players were already playing in Sydney, but were refused permission by their clubs to play for the Lions. Both hookers were injured, and John Gray played there in the second test, while Roger Millward played on the wing.

This match, at the Sydney Cricket Ground, saw the makeshift Lions team win a controversial victory. Jim did a high tackle on Australian second-row Gary Stevens, although he was not cautioned by referee Keith Page. The history of South Sydney, *Glory Days*, says that "Early in the match Stevens was knocked senseless in a high tackle attributed to fiery Welshman Jim Mills; Stevens said later he did not remember the rest of the game."

The next scrum saw a huge brawl. John Gray was kicked in the face and had to leave the field to have stitches, although he returned to the action 12 minutes later. Lions prop Jimmy Thomson was knocked out by a punch, but played on. Tries from Eric Chisnall and Colin Dixon, both converted by Gray, gave the Lions a 10–3 half-time lead. A further try from Gill early in the second half, again converted by Gray, gave the Lions a 15–3 lead, and although Australia came back near the end the Lions won 16–11 to level the series.

The third test was two weeks later, again at the SCG. Jim missed the game, having injured his knee in the second test. The Australians, clearly shaken by their defeat, dropped seven players for the match. Five of the Lions played with pain-killing injections, and although they were 16–10 ahead at the break, lost 22–18. Alan Whiticker and Ian Collis comment in their history of test matches in Australia that the home team were "aided by a spate of penalties by referee Keith Page." Great Britain were only given two penalties in the second half.

Had the Lions had a fully-fit team, or been able to use some of the British international players based in Sydney, they could have won. As it was, the Australians held onto the Ashes. Whiticker and Collis say that it had been "one of the closest Ashes contests on record" and that Great Britain were "courageous in defeat."

The tourists crossed the Tasman Sea to New Zealand, and a further eight matches. Jim recalls "good, hard games" in New Zealand and in particular the match in Rotorua against the Maori. "We were well looked after, and I always remember the singing after the game." Jim missed the first test, when Great Britain had lost 13–8, and Robert Gate comments that "the worst of their problems was an astonishing display of refereeing from John Percival. He caned the Lions with 22 penalties and awarded them only 10..."

Jim returned for the second test in Christchurch, when the Lions squad had only 17 fit players. With four minutes left the Lions were behind, but tries from Les Dyl and Chris Hesketh, both converted by Gray, saw Great Britain win 17–8. A week later, the Lions won comfortably, 20–0, to take the series. On the tour, Jim started 15 matches, made one appearance from the bench, and scored two tries, against North Coast and Riverina.

Controversy! Tackling Gary Stevens in the Australia versus Great Britain second test in 1974.

The Welsh players in the 1974 Lions squad. Back: Dave Willicombe, Colin Dixon, Jim, Maurice Richards; front: John Bevan and David Watkins.

Left: Jim with a professional boxer from Argentina the team met in their hotel in Brisbane.

Middle: Making friends in Brisbane.

Bottom: Gotcha! Stopping an Australian attack by Ron Coote. (Courtesy *Rugby League Journal*)

Looking back, Jim says that "I think it's a pity that today's players don't do the tours that we did. Being on a Great Britain tour was a highlight of my career. We were away for three months, and it was the top level for any player. A whole part of the tradition and history of the game has been destroyed. Pubs in Australia, especially in the country areas, have the big long photos of the touring teams on display. All that has stopped, it is a big loss for the game. Australia and New Zealand used to look forward to the tours, especially in the country areas. Local players could say 'I played against Great Britain.' It was great for them."

In 1977, Jim was selected for the Lions World Cup squad to play in Australia and New Zealand, but had to withdraw at the last minute due to a hernia operation. He had been included in the team photo. However, this did avoid some controversy over whether the New Zealanders would play against him following the Greengrass incident in 1975.

In 1978, the Australians came on tour. There had been controversy over their team selection, with only three Queenslanders in their squad. Jim was now aged 34, and while he would have expected to play against the tourists for Wales and Widnes, a Great Britain recall seemed unlikely.

Peter Fox was now the Great Britain coach, but he could not prevent the Australians winning the first test 15–9 at Central Park. It was a match "riddled with nastiness" according to Robert Gate. Great Britain team manager Harry Womersley accused the Australians of biting; the Australians complained about the home team's high tackling. Steve Nash broke his nose and Roger Millward was concussed. For the Australians, Rod Reddy was kicked in the head.

Peter Fox gave a pledge before the second test of 'no violence' which was viewed with some scepticism by the Australians, especially when Great Britain announced a front row of Jim, Tony Fisher and Brian Lockwood. Brad Boxall of the Australian Rugby League Week said that the Lions pack "looked like refugees from the Yorkshire Old Men's Home". The British press, more generously, called them the 'Dad's Army' team, after the popular television comedy based on the wartime Home Guard.

Robert Gate comments in *The Struggle for the Ashes*: "Much to the delight of the British fans and the chagrin of the Aussies, it was the display of the geriatric Mills, Fisher and Lockwood which formed the basis for a remarkable British victory... Mills was simply the "Big Jim" Mills fans either loved or hated, prepared to take on the entire Kangaroo pack and thereby distract them from playing too much football."

The ages of the Lions front row totalled 101, and Jim recalls that "We gave them a shock in the second test and beat them. A crowd of 26,447, the biggest in England for five years apart from the Challenge Cup final, saw the Lions lead 11–4 at half-time. With 10 minutes left the Lions looked to be comfortably home with an 18–4 lead, but the Australians scored two converted tries to make the final score 18–14. One incident involved Jim and Rod Reddy. Ian Heads comments in *The Kangaroos*: "In a sensational incident in the second half big Jim Mills head-butted Reddy, claiming that he had been bitten in a tackle."

Jim's recollection of the incident is slightly different: "Rod Reddy did attempt to bite me when I put my hand around his head to drag him down. There was a bit of biting going on that tour so when I felt his teeth on my hand I responded before he sank his teeth in. I told the ref that he had bitten me and I was holding my hand. Luckily he did not look at my hand because I had no mark on it.

I remember Ronnie Barrett, the Great Britain physio coming on to treat me and I told him to hop it because he had not managed to bite me and we were awarded a penalty, so it was retribution before the intended act."

With the series evenly balanced at one match each, another huge crowd squeezed into Headingley for the final test. Jim recalls that "Brian Lockwood, who had been playing well, was out injured, one or two things went wrong and they beat us easily. If everyone had been fit, we would have run them close." At one time in the second half, the Australians were 20–0 ahead, and won 23–6 in the end. The win at Odsal was Great Britain's last against Australia until 1988.

Jim enjoyed working with Peter Fox: "Peter was a good coach, and well respected in the game. He had a lot of good ideas, said what he felt, and was unfortunate not to be the coach on the 1979 Lions tour." Always prepared to try something different, Fox had read the poem *The Indispensable Man* by Saxon White Kessinger to the team before the match. After the game, Fox simply commented that "everything had gone to plan".

The 1978 Great Britain squad. Back: Jim, S. Wright, J. Holmes, J. Joyner, G. Nicholls, J. Bevan, P. Rose, J. Atkinson, P. Lowe; middle: F. Robinson (kitman), A. Fisher, L. Casey, P. Hogan, V. Farrar, G. Fairbairn, Smith, S. Norton, B. Lockwood; front: L. Dyl, R. Barritt (physio), K. Mumby, H. Womersley (manager), R. Millward, D. Gemmell (Assistant manager), S. Nash, P. Fox (coach), G. Stephens.

With Peter Fox and Tony Fisher before the Dad's Army test in 1978.

The front row from the 1978 'Dad's Army' test: Brian Lockwood, Tony Fisher and Jim. Their combined ages were over 100.

Before the 'Dad's Army' test.

With Brian Lockwood (10) and referee Mick Naughton in the 'Dad's Army' test. (Courtesy *Rugby League Journal*)

Jim was one of a number of older players who were chosen for the 1979 Lions tour. He recalls: "I was still playing well, but had trouble with my right knee. A lot of the players in that squad were over the hill in international terms, but we were the best players available at that time. Not many youngsters were coming through. The hard grounds were an additional problem for the older players, and my knee swelled up to twice its normal size. I had to come home, along with Steve Nash, Roger Millward, Tommy Martyn and the captain, Doug Laughton. George Nicholls took over as captain." John Burke, George Fairbairn and David Topliss joined the squad as replacements, but the Lions lost the Ashes series 3–0, scoring just 18 points and conceding 87.

However, the controversy after the Greengrass incident was still there for Jim. On 14 June, the *Daily Mirror* reported that the International Board had confirmed that he would not be allowed to play in New Zealand, following his life ban by New Zealand. However, injury forced Jim to come home before the squad headed for New Zealand, so the matter was never put to the test.

Jim played in the first test, which was lost 35–0. It was, at the time, the biggest winning margin in an Ashes test on Australian soil, and Great Britain's worst result since 1963. Jim came off after 25 minutes with a knee injury. Whiticker and Collis comment that "The 1979 Lions were completely outclassed in Australia, although they did win the test series in New Zealand, 2–1." They do say that many of the players had been playing club matches right up until they left for the tour, after a bad winter in England; and seven players joined the tour late, with coach Eric Ashton, whose daughter had been in a car accident. Of the first test, they say: "Australia's win was helped immeasurably by one of the most inept tackling displays ever produced by a Great Britain side"

A young Wally Lewis played against the Lions for Queensland, and Adrian McGregor's biography, *Forever the King*, outlines how Jim helped keep the youngster out of trouble: "Wally raced in during one brawl and suddenly felt himself being withdrawn by the scruff of his jersey. He turned around, half cocking his fist and confronted Jim Mills... Wally expected to be knocked into the middle of next week, but Mills said, 'Don't go in there, son.' Wally nodded his head, 'Righto, no, I'll break it up.' He and Mills separated the brawlers. Five minutes later there was another blue and Mills was in the middle of it thumping players right, left and centre."

The 1979 Lions squad. (Courtesy *Rugby League Journal*)

However in the book *Legends of Australian Sport*, it says that after extracting Lewis from the brawl, "Mills flattened the Queensland captain Greg Vievers with a haymaker that Muhammad Ali would have been proud of. Wally was surprised as Mills's unexpected concern: 'Gee, thanks mate'." Both books say that the match was against Brisbane. In fact, Jim did not play in that match, which was two days after the first test, when he had gone off with the knee injury that finished his tour. He did play against Queensland. Lewis came on as a substitute in both matches.

Jim played just five games, although one positive memory was that "In my last game, one of the country ones, I captained the side. But I was hobbling around. Really I shouldn't have gone on the tour. With my knee injury the hard grounds were always going to cause me problems."

On 20 June, in his column in the *Daily Mirror*, written with Arthur Brooks, Jim said that he was "absolutely shattered" that the injury to his right knee, which was "swollen up to almost football-size" meant that he would have to come home. John Burke was flown out as a replacement. Jim's last game was against Monaro at Queanbeyan on Sunday 8 July. With the Lions having played – and beaten – New South Wales the day before, he captained a makeshift side that won 21–7 in front of 2,944 fans.

Even then, in a country game, Jim nearly got into trouble. In his *Daily Mirror* column, he told Arthur Brooks that he was "almost choked with pride" to be leading out Great Britain. He said that the referee had cautioned him 'a few times' and then one of the Monaro forwards pole-

With Steve Nash, Doug Laughton and Tommy Martyn (Senior) in 1979.

axed Steve Evans, one of the Lions' youngsters. Jim commented that "It is no secret that I never like seeing my team-mates get clobbered, particularly the young ones. I had to wait a few minutes before the chance came to repay the compliment. When it did, that Monaro back-rower was suddenly in a horizontal position and seeing stars." The touch judge rushed on, and the referee threatened to send Jim off. Jim told him "You can't do that ref. I'm the captain." Jim stayed on the pitch, and his cheek had prevented him being sent off on his final Great Britain appearance. Maybe if that interpretation of the laws had been applied more widely, Jim would have been captain more often.

The Australians won the second test the next week 24–16, but had been 17–4 up at the break, and the Lions humiliation was completed in the third test, which the home side won 28–2, although they did win the series in New Zealand. It was a warning of what was to come in the 1980s, when the Australian 'Invincibles' dominated the 1982 series; and were heralded as one of the greatest rugby league teams ever. Great Britain would wait until 1988 for another test match Ashes victory.

10. A proud Welshman

Rugby league has longstanding links with Wales. Even before the split in 1895 which formed the Northern Union, players moved from South Wales to play their rugby in the north of England. Over the years, hundreds of players abandoned rugby union and their amateur status to go north and play rugby league. Many stayed in the north and became an important part of local communities. At some clubs, at times almost half the first team would be Welsh, as players contacted their former team mates back home to encourage them to come north.

Rugby union in South Wales has a strong working class base, and players were moving to similar communities in the north, based on heavy industry and coal mining. There were, of course, recruits from union from the other home nations, especially the borders region in Scotland, but – with some exceptions – union was a more middle class game, and there was less economic need to play professionally.

Jim left South Wales in 1964, almost 50 years ago, and has lived for most of his life in the north of England. But his Welsh identity is still very strong. During the work on this book, he attended a St David's Day reunion with 35 past Welsh rugby league players; although he says that as they are getting older the singing is not as good as it used to be. They meet up twice a year. He recalls his Welsh origins with great pride, and one of his regrets in his life is that he never played for the Welsh rugby union team. His distinctive Mercedes car has a Wales sticker on the back, showing his roots. He does some after-dinner speaking, and particularly enjoys his trips to South Wales, where he has spoken at Cardiff, Llanelli, Newport and Swansea in recent years.

Jim was the first chairman of the Welsh rugby league past players association, with David Watkins as secretary, Roy Mathias as treasurer, and the great Trevor Foster as president. He recalls their first annual dinner, with former greats such as Gus Risman in attendance. Cliff Morgan spoke at a dinner, as did Brian Thomas, the former Neath and Wales forward. Sadly, the association was dissolved a few years ago, because of decreasing numbers. Since rugby union went open, there has been little incentive for Welsh players at the top level to switch from union to league. Why leave home and play a new game where you may not be successful and can earn as much playing rugby union anyway? However, the game now has a strong base in Wales, with two semi-professional clubs and well-established amateur, student and school competitions.

From the sport's first international matches until the early 1950s, the Welsh team was an important part of the international set-up. But in the early 1950s, with the flow of talent from the Valleys drying up, it was disbanded to help develop the Great Britain team for the 1954 World Cup. With the plug also being pulled soon afterwards on the 'Other Nationalities' side, international rugby league in the northern hemisphere was reduced to Great Britain and France.

However, the movement of players to rugby league never fully stopped, and by 1968, it was decided to revive the Welsh side, playing against England and France in a European championship. For Jim this was very significant, because it gave him a chance to play at international level, and saw him taking part in two of the great matches in Wales's post-war history, the team's return to play in Wales in 1975 at Swansea, and the 'Battle of Brisbane' against the old enemy, England, in the 1975 World Championship.

Jim was not selected for the two matches in the 1968–69 season, but made his senior international debut in either code against England at Headingley on 18 October 1969. He recalls his international debut in rugby league: "Playing for the Wales Rugby League team was my first senior representative appearance. It was all lads I knew, former rugby union players. It was a great moment for me, like being back at home." Wales were 13–12 ahead at half-time, but went down 40–23 after England took control in the second half.

Five days later, Jim made his second appearance for his country. Although the RFL had revived the Welsh team, they were not yet playing in Wales, so faced France at Salford. However, Jim did not finish the game: "In October 1969 I played against France. Georges Allieres was propping against me. I butted him in the scrum and got sent off. He had a big bandage put on his head. After I retired I was in France with Kel Coslett. George was walking down the road, saw me and hugged me. 'Big Jim' he said, and introduced me to his wife."

Jim returned to action in the next match, when Wales travelled to Perpignan for the return match against the French. They won 15–11, and referee Dickie Thomas was attacked by supporters after the game. A month later, they returned to Headingley for their 'home' match against England, and went down 26–7. However, these four international appearances, along with his consistent displays for Bradford, led to Jim's selection for the 1970 Lions tour, although he subsequently withdrew from it to sign for North Sydney.

Jim played with some very talented Welsh players. He recalls: "Some of the Welsh players who stand out from my time are Colin Dixon, Terry Price, John Mantle, David Watkins, David Willicombe, Ronnie Hill, Kel Coslett, Tony Fisher, Paul Woods, Roy Mathias, John Bevan, Maurice Richards, Mike Nicholas, Clive Sullivan, Bobby Wanbon, John Warlow, Bill Francis, Mick Murphy, Eddie Cunningham, Glyn Shaw, Brian Butler, Peter Rowe, Dickie Evans, Frank Wilson and Peter Banner. David Watkins was very like Jonathan Davies. I played with David at Salford briefly. He was very fast. In a seven-a-side tournament he could win it on his own. No one could catch him. He wasn't big, but he could run backwards as fast as forwards."

Soon after winning his fourth cap, Jim headed off to Australia to play for North Sydney, and the RFL decided to once again focus on the Great Britain side, with the 1970 and 1972 World Cups in mind. However, in 1975 it was agreed to stage a 'World Championship' in Australia and New Zealand in June, with return matches in England and Wales in October and November. And a French proposal that England and Wales would play, instead of Great Britain, was accepted.

To prepare for the tournament, the European Championship was revived. On 16 February 1975, after an absence from the country of almost 25 years, Wales played France in Swansea. The match was played at the St Helens ground which had staged some great matches for Wales in the 1940s. The match programme cheekily listed the rugby union antecedents of the Welsh team, although only four had won full international honours, 12 had played club or schools rugby union in Wales. Two, Bill Francis and Peter Banner, were from a rugby league background, but qualified through Welsh heritage. It also included articles about amateur, university and schools rugby league, giving out a message that the northern sport was not solely a 'professional' game.

The Welsh fans flocked to the ground to see the former union stars. The attendance was given as 15,000; but the officials opened the gates to let people in from queues outside the ground as the game started; the crowd was certainly over 20,000. Jim was described in the programme as a "World renowned tackle breaker". He was in a fierce front row with Tony Fisher and John Mantle.

RUGBY LEAGUE
INTERNATIONAL TRIANGULAR TOURNAMENT

WALES
V
FRANCE

ICH DIEN

St. Helens — Swansea
February 16th 1975 - Kick Off 3pm

Official Programme   Price 10p

Left: The heroes return. Wales's first real home match since the early 1950s.

Below: The 1975 Wales World Championship squad. (Courtesy *Rugby League Journal*) Back: Clive Sullivan, Mike Nicholas, Eddie Cunningham, Kel Coslett, Tony Fisher, Roy Mathias, Glyn Turner; middle: John Malpas (phyiso), Dick Evans, Brian Butler, Bobby Wanbon, Jim, David Willicombe, Colin Dixon, John Mantle, Les Pearce (coach); front: Frank Wilson, Bill Francis, Peter Banner, Ron Simpson (manager), David Watkins (Capt.), David Treasure, Peter Rowe.

France were 3–2 up at the break, but the Welsh side dominated the second half to win 21–8. Jim capped his first appearance in Wales for almost 11 years with a try. He recalls that great night: "A massive crowd turned out to see the old rugby union players. I scored in the corner, and leaning on the fence were my cousins from Aberdare, who had come to watch. There was a marvellous atmosphere. They had to open the gates to get the crowd in; there were so many waiting outside. John Bevan, who played for the British Lions rugby union team, had moved to rugby league by then and scored twice for us."

Ten days later, Wales faced England at Salford. They couldn't repeat the form they showed against the French, and lost 12–8, although they recovered from a 10–3 half-time deficit. Jim again played at prop, but was sent off. However, the World Championship was not far away, and Wales would get their revenge.

Jim missed Wales's first match of the World Championship, a 14–7 defeat against France in Toulouse. A strange schedule meant that instead of playing England in Wales, they would face the old enemy in Brisbane, on 10 June 1975, a match that became known as the 'Battle of Brisbane'.

Jim says that "It was one of those games, playing against team mates and friends, for your country. Alex Murphy had been on television the night before; when he was asked about the Welsh team, he said that 'none of them are good enough to get in the England team'. That set the match up, when he said that, everyone was a bit bitter. It was a very violent game, and Mick Morgan, the England hooker was knocked unconscious and was carried off on three occasions. I admired him for keeping on coming back, although he may not have known what he was doing. There were a lot of bust ups, it was a hard fought game and we came out on top. The Aussies enjoyed it. They were playing us the following weekend. We didn't have a chance to recover and were still tired. If we hadn't beaten England, they would have won the World Championship.

Les Pearce was our coach. He was a great coach, well respected by all the boys, and did a great job for us when we beat England. I am still in contact with him. The team manager was Ronnie Simpson from Castleford. That was a very good Welsh team, maybe aging a little bit, but still a great side. It wasn't a shock to us to beat England, they had a good team, but we were good enough to beat them."

League Publications' book on the *Rugby League World Cup* describes the game as a "vicious, brutal encounter" and says that the Welsh won both the match, with tries from David Treasure and Clive Sullivan, and the "succession of all-in brawls". The report goes on: "It seemed like each side had been saving everything for this grudge match against the traditional enemy. Referee Don Lancashire said after the game that he would have been completely justified in sending off every single player in their 'boots and all' clash. The Welsh hardly used their skilful backs... Instead it was left to their rugged pack, with Jim Mills, Tony Fisher, Bobby Wanbon and John Mantle to the fore... when the English fell into the trap of getting into the fisticuffs, Wales turned on some fine rugby."

Four days later, Wales had to face Australia, and lost 30–13. With some older players in the squad, Wales did not show the same fight that they had against England. Jim recalls: "The Welsh boys did not think it was fair that we had to play Australia only four days after the hard match against England, which put us at a big disadvantage as the Aussies were nice and fresh. We still had knocks from the England game, and didn't have a big squad."

Wales then flew to New Zealand, and played Wellington, the West Coast and Canterbury before facing New Zealand in Auckland on 28 June. Jim recalls: "In New Zealand we played in Greymouth. We had matches before the test matches and we only had a small squad, but we won both of them. Broadhurst had kicked one of our players in the head and Mike Nicholas had been carried off. This was in a midweek match before the test match."

Once again, Jim ran into controversy: "There were two incidents on this part of the tour which I received very bad press about, the games against West Coast at Greymouth, on 22 June 1975, and two days later on 24 June 1975 against Canterbury at Christchurch. Both games were very violent, which seemed to be arranged for us before we played the test against New Zealand the following weekend. In the game against West Coast, there were many nasty incidents, one of which resulted in me punching their second-row forward John Pattinson, which resulted in him being stretchered off the field. The next day I received a very bad press, but nothing was mentioned about the stick that we took. I remember Bill Francis, our stand-off, had a big gash in his head after being kicked. We then travelled to Christchurch and another very violent encounter with Canterbury. I was put on the bench after the bad press coverage of the previous game, because we had a test match coming up and they didn't want me to be sent off.

But just after half time, Mike Nicholas was carried off injured, and I had to go on. It was not long before I was involved in an incident with Mark Broadhurst, the Canterbury second-row forward, which resulted in him being stretchered off and taken to hospital. After the game our coach Les Pearce went to the hospital to visit him and wish him well. Again, I received a very bad press. I was sorry about the incidents, but we were taking plenty of punishment in both games, and these incidents definitely stopped the violence."

Mike Nicholas recalls: "We played together for Wales. There was a lot of respect for Jim, and he was sociable off the pitch. But when things got tough, he got going. I remember him reducing the French front-row to cardboard cut-outs. It was very physical; he didn't do things in halves. When we were on tour in Australia and New Zealand, ambulances followed us.

At one match, on the west coast, the ambulance had to come onto the pitch to take one of their players off. And, of course, Jim played in the 'Battle of Brisbane' game against England. We were playing against our club team-mates, but no quarter was given. That defeat cost England the World Cup, and Jim stirred them up."

Not surprisingly, Wales lost to New Zealand 13–8, and then played another two matches against Auckland and the New Zealand Maori team before returning home. Jim scored a try and says that "This was a close, hard-fought game, which we could have won."

Wales scored two tries to the home team's one, but five goals from Warren Collicoat won it for the Kiwis. Murray Eade was sent off in the second half for a high tackle on Bill Francis; but then eight minutes from the end David Treasure was sent off for Wales.

The matches in New Zealand, both against the local sides and the World Championship game against the Kiwis are an important part of the background to the incident-filled match when the teams met again at Swansea on 2 November. It was one that blighted the rest of Jim's rugby league career.

Mayhem! Australia versus Wales World Cup 1975 at Sydney Cricket Ground.

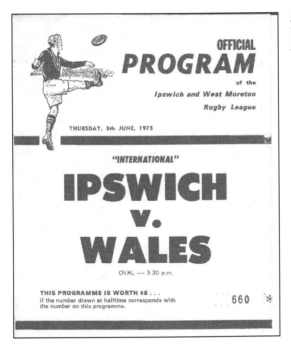

OFFICIAL

PROGRAM

of the

Ipswich and West Moreton

Rugby League

THURSDAY, 5th JUNE, 1975

"INTERNATIONAL"

IPSWICH
V.
WALES

OVAL — 3.30 p.m.

THIS PROGRAMME IS WORTH $5 . . .
If the number drawn at halftime corresponds with
the number on this programme.

660

Jim scored a try in Wales's 35–13 win in June 1975.

Jim scoring against New Zealand in the 1975 World Championship.

What did you say? Jim, John Mantle and Artie Beetson; Wales versus Australia at Swansea, World Championship 1975. This was the start of an all-in brawl. (Courtesy *Rugby League Journal*)

The tournament resumed in September, when England beat Wales 22–16 at Warrington. Jim missed this game, but he was selected for their final two games, against Australia and New Zealand. On Sunday 19 October, 11,112 fans were at the Vetch Field in Swansea to see Australia beat Wales 18–6. Wales gave a good account of themselves, and were 6–2 ahead in the first half, before the Australians came back to win 18–6. However, it was Jim's clashes with Artie Beetson that took the headlines. Jim recalls: "Then we played the Australians at Swansea. It was a close game, we could have won. It was our best chance to beat them. I had a fight with Artie Beetson on the touchline. I was punched in the back of the head by Greg Veivers [Phil Veivers' brother], who was one of their forwards, while I was holding Beetson. As the fight broke up I realised it was him. Retribution wasn't long coming; he was carried from the field 10 minutes later." *The History of the Rugby League World Cup* outlines: "The Swansea encounter was another brutal encounter, a feature of so many of Wales's matches during the championship. Three major brawls broke out as referee Percival failed to dampen the players' fire. One melee rolled off the pitch and into the grandstand at Vetch Field where several officials, including Australia's coach Graeme Langlands joined in."

Jim and Artie Beetson had history, after Beetson had been outraged and kicked Jim after Jim had knocked out Gary Stevens in the second test on the 1974 Lions tour. In his autobiography, Beetson recalled the Swansea match: "This was a tournament of tough football, none more brutal than when we went to Swansea to play the Welsh. The match was memorable for two things. In the football sense it was Ian Schubert's game, as the strong, young Easts winger scoring three brilliant tries in an 18–6 Australian win. But the game is remembered just as much for the brawls which took place as referee Percival struggled to keep control. No blue was fiercer than the one that spilled across the touchline and almost to the fence and during which the Welsh coach Les Pearce clocked our second-rower Ray Higgs, gaining himself some unwelcome headlines."

However, Beetson was not the only Australian forward who was after Jim. In Malcolm Andrews's *Hardmen*, he quotes Ken Arthurson saying that Terry Randall "hit Mills so hard I thought he would break him in two. Mills was a giant of a man... so big and so tough. But Terry hammered him, leaving him gasping for breath; the timing of that tackle was perfect." Randall recalls: "I'd played against Mills when he was at North Sydney, so I knew what to expect... a powerhouse. But I got on top of him." Reading this now, Jim does not dispute being tackled hard, but disputes that he was gasping for breath. The tackle wasn't that memorable for Jim.

Two weeks later, Wales returned to the Vetch Field to play New Zealand. Only 2,645 saw the match, which Wales won 25–24. This was another bad-tempered physical match. Jim outlines: "Then we beat New Zealand at Swansea, when I was sent off. It was a very close game and could have gone either way. I could have cost us the game, but it was near the end when I was sent off."

Jim was sent off for stamping on John Greengrass, an incident which caused him problems for the rest of his international career. That incident is covered fully elsewhere in this book. Jack Winstanley and Malcolm Ryding comment in the *John Player Rugby League Yearbook 1976–77*: "All the free-scoring that featured in this game was sadly overshadowed by some ugly physical incidents that culminated in the dismissal of Jim Mills... Two New Zealand players, full-back Collicoat and stand-off Jarvis, were injured during the game, while Wales's Francis (cheek) and Fisher (arm) were also in the wars." In *The Kiwis*, John Coffey and Bernie Wood's history of New Zealand's international matches, the authors are not surprisingly very critical of some of the Welsh play. But they admit that "It was not all one way. Before spraining his ankle and limping off, Jarvis might have been dismissed for punching Welsh stand-off Bill Francis..."

One of the New Zealand forwards was Kurt Sorensen, who Jim later got to know well: "I remember playing against a young Kurt Sorensen, who later played for Widnes and was a partner with me in the nightclubs. He made his debut in the 1975 World Championship and later we talked about it. He said that he was nervous and sitting in the dressing room before the game. He was told 'Don't get involved with the physical side, just play rugby. Mills and Fisher are mental!' He was a good player, as was his brother Dane, who also played for New Zealand. Overall, that was a good competition, with some good battles."

Jim next pulled on the red shirt of Wales in January 1977, against England at Headingley in the European Championship. Jim was playing for Workington, but wanted to move back to a Lancashire club, and was part of a Welsh team that beat the old enemy 6–2. Once again, Wales played both their matches away from home, and three weeks later Wales travelled to Toulouse and went down 13–2 to France, who beat England in the tournament's final match to take the title. The World Cup, played that summer in Australia and New Zealand, reverted to Great Britain playing instead of Wales and England, and was a shorter tournament, rather than the elongated extravaganza of 1975. Jim was selected for Great Britain, but missed out through injury. For once he avoided controversy, because the Kiwis had said that they would not play against him, or let him play in New Zealand.

In 1977–78, the RFL again decided that Wales's home matches should be played in the north of England. On 15 January, Jim lined up with Widnes colleagues Paul Woods and Glyn Shaw at Naughton Park to play France. A crowd of 9,502 came to see a Wales team with 12 Lancashire-based players in their squad, and witnessed a 29–7 win, and a try from Jim. But at the end of the season, on 28 May, against England at Knowsley Road, Jim recalls that: "It was boiling hot and they ran riot". England won 60–13, scoring 14 tries, to take the title.

The 1978–79 season saw Jim make his final two appearances for Wales. A disappointing crowd of 4,250 saw Wales go down narrowly to the Australian tourists at Swansea. Jim remembers that "It was very close, nothing in it. The Aussies had a scrum near our line; they threw the ball into the second row and scored from it. It cost us the game." Jim and Australian forward Rod Reddy clashed regularly during the game, which featured 37 penalties. Had David Watkins kicked three penalties in the second half, the Australians could have been beaten. In *The Kangaroos*, a history of Australian touring sides, Ian Heads comments: "...An 'elderly' band of Welshmen went close to wrecking a few reputations when the Australians travelled to Swansea...The Welsh team... cleverly slowed the pace of the game and stretched the Australians to near breaking point..."

Jim's final match for Wales was on 16 March 1979, a home fixture, but again played at Naughton Park. A crowd of just over 5,000 saw Wales hold England to 5–5 at half-time before going down 15–7.

The match was memorable for a brawl resulting from a scrum collapsing. Jim recalls that "Tommy Cunningham, who was our hooker, got a kick in the face. I though Harry Beverley, who was a huge prop from Workington, had done it, so I hit him, and he had a terrible gash under his eye. Afterwards, Beverley denied that he had been responsible. Beverley went off, and Tommy Cunningham had to be substituted as well. Mike Nicholas replaced him, and played well. Because the match was at Widnes, our physio, Frank Tobin was on duty, and at training that week he told me he'd 'put loads of stitches' into Harry Beverley."

Overall for Wales, Jim won 15 caps in almost 10 years. He played in almost two-thirds of the matches Wales played between 1968 and 1979. He scored three tries and was sent off twice.

David Watkins was both a team-mate of Jim's for Wales, and his coach. He has a lot of respect for Jim: "Not many accept Jim for what he was, especially in his middle to late years, a very good international class forward. Jim was not just an all punching and kneeing, big awesome man; he could play the game with the best. Make no mistake there was much more to him than a fighting man, Jim Mills was a great forward. He was a major player for his beloved Wales. His partnership with Tony Fisher both for Great Britain and Wales even had the Australians quaking in their boots. He would take nothing from the Aussies. If they hit him or any team mate he would return the compliment with a bonus, he feared no one. He was indeed a talented rugby league forward, one of the best. He was a great mate on the field to all his team mates and a wonderful character on the tours he made for both Britain and Wales. A great comic and his rendition of *the Scottish Soldier* was heard all over the rugby league playing world.

Wales squad training in Widnes in the late 1970s. Back: Doctor, Mike Nicholas, Roy Mathias, Peter Rowe, Jim, Ron Simpson (manager), Glyn Shaw, Mel James, Colin Dixon, David Willicombe, Kel Coslett (coach); front: Gordon Pritchard, Clive Jones, Paul Woods, Bill Francis, Eddie Cunningham, Clive Sullivan, John Risman, Dickie Evans.

Sure Jim had a short fuse, but that fuse was ignited on most occasions when seeing his much smaller team mates being bullied by bigger opposition forwards. As Jim's international coach I found that he did exactly as he was asked and there have been only fewer better 'enforcers' in the game's history."

Another former Welsh player with upmost respect for Jim is Kel Coslett: "I have known Jim Mills for many years, played with him at international level and against him at club level. I coached him while he and I represented Wales together. We have been and still are very good friends. But my respect for Jim would be just as strong if we were not good friends. We were mates in rugby football and in business because I represented the brewery who supplied Jim at his two clubs for quite a few years.

He was a top class act as a player, tremendous agility and rugby football ability for such a huge man and his pace for such a big man had to be seen to be believed. While being accepted amongst the players of his time as being 'special', not many spectators realised what a great team man Jim was. It was in his nature to 'look after' and protect his team mates. Because of this Jim was vulnerable to the wiles of experienced shrewd tough men who would foul a smaller member of Jim's team to play on Jim's one weakness, retaliation. But he was no fool; sometimes he would wait his time and take retribution when the time was right. Of course no man can hold back if something really bad is done to a team mate and in these times Jim was an awesome sight.

If he saw a player on his side being attacked, he would move heaven and earth to get to the aggressor and introduce his own kind of vengeance. Referees universally missed the original foul, but always caught Jim. Because of his reputation, Jim was many times called out by the referee and dismissed from the field for nothing. Hence, he did not receive the full credit for his superb ability. As a wide runner he was awesome, devastating. Because he was Jim Mills he was credited with knocking players down in retaliation, he was not totally accepted as the fast moving, huge bulk of bone and muscle who could blitz defences. But away from the rugby field Jim is a pure gentleman to whom nothing is too much trouble for him to do for you. A tremendous friend and I am honoured to call him so. I can't think of a more fitting tribute to Jim if I say quite honestly, he would always be in my team."

In 1991, the RFL decided to revive the Wales international team. Following Jonathan Davies's move to Widnes, other union players had also come north, and the team was viable again. They returned to action against Papua New Guinea at Swansea, and Jim became team manager. He recalls: "Clive Griffiths was a good coach and the team were doing well. Maurice Lindsay, who was chief executive of the RFL by then, told me that if we beat Papua New Guinea and France, we would be given a place in the 1995 World Cup. We had a good team. Apart from Jonathan, there was John Devereux, Paul Moriarty and David Young. Then they had a meeting in Australia of the International Board and decided that Wales would not be included/ Clive Griffiths was very upset, and I resigned in protest. They asked Trevor Foster to take it on, but I'd told Trevor why I'd resigned, and he wouldn't do it. He was very supportive of the team. He would come into the dressing room before the matches, and offer to help to rub the players down.

Anyway, Mike Nicholas took over as team manager and did a good job. And the team was reinstated in the World Cup and did very well."

Apart from playing for Wales and Great Britain, Jim also played once for Other Nationalities. Until the early 1950s, this team played England, Wales and France in an international championship, and included some of the sport's legends. However, the team that Jim played for was in the County Championship. Jim played once, against Yorkshire at Craven Park on 18 September 1974. The home side won 22–15.

Playing for Wales against Australia in Swansea in 1975.

Welsh rugby league greats signing *Happy Birthday* to Les Pearce.
From left: Garfield Owen, Kel Coslett, Les Pearce, Jim,
Billy Boston, John Thorley.

11. Count to three

Jim's total of 20 sendings off is unimaginable in professional rugby league today. Today, at the top level of the game, sendings-off are rare. Even players being sent to the 'sin-bin' is not that common. Referees do have the option to put a player' on report' if they feel they have not seen an alleged incident, or had a clear view. This has been one factor in reducing the number of sendings-off, but the main one is the far more regimented and disciplined approach by coaches to how their teams play the game. Also, in the modern game players are often warned or suspended for incidents in matches by the disciplinary committee, which have not merited a red card by the referee.

However, just as this chapter was being written, early in the 2013 Super League season, there were three sendings off, two for the same player, Justin Poore of Wakefield Trinity Wildcats. His frustrated coach, Richard Agar, said that he had no argument with the sending off, which was for a punch, and added "You just can't do things like that. It's not the 1980s," (Dave Hadfield report, *The Independent*, 8 April 2013), reflecting the change in attitude. Today, some teams go a complete season without a player receiving the red card.

Barrie McDermott, known for being a 'hard' forward in the modern era, only was sent off six times in British first team matches, the last one in 2002; although he was sin-binned three times, once in 2005 and twice in 2006 before he retired at the end of that season.

Looking at the *Opta* statistics for Super League, in the *League Express 2012–13 Annual*, the worst team for conceding penalties was the Widnes Vikings, but even their figure was under 10 a match. The team with the best record, Castleford Tigers, conceded just over 7 penalties a match. There are eight categories of penalty recorded, but 'fighting' and 'punching' are not mentioned; presumably subsumed within 'foul play'. The biggest category is for 'interference', followed by 'foul play'. Tony Collins shows in his book, *Rugby League in Twentieth Century Britain*, that in the 1970–71 season, roughly halfway through Jim's career, there were 142 sendings-off in the professional game, 70 of which were for punching or fighting; very different from today.

If a time-traveller league fan could use some Tardis-like machine to travel from the 1960s or 1970s to watch today's Super League, they would – just about – recognise it as the same game they had left behind. There are still 13 players on each side on the pitch, and points are scored through tries and goals. But they would also find huge changes. It would take another book to cover them adequately; they would include: full-time professionalism at the top level; universal and detailed television coverage, including video-replays in televised matches to assist the referee in making decisions; far better fitness levels, diets for players and 'sports science' analysing their fitness; different playing strips and boots; grounds which may be on the same site but with todays' vastly improved facilities and safety; a different scoring system; competitive scrums; full-time referees at the top level; substitutes; and finally, fundamental changes to the game's approach to discipline. This level of change is not just in rugby league. A similar list could be drawn up for association football, rugby union and cricket.

Australian rugby league writer Malcolm Andrews recognises the changes in the Introduction to his book *Hardmen,* published in 2012: "Whenever rugby league fans get to talking about their favourite game in the local pub or club, the conversation will invariably turn to 'the good old days'. Or maybe that should be 'the bad old days', when violence on the football pitch largely went unchecked. Stiff-arm tackles delivered with the sole aim of maiming the opposition player. Head-butts designed to smash noses and fracture cheekbones. Spear tackles that drove players headfirst into the turf with never a thought that the consequence could be a broken neck. And more fisticuffs than on a Monday night at the old Sydney Stadium at Rushcutters Bay [a famous boxing venue]."

The introduction to a similar book published in 1994, *Hitmen* by Tony Adams, which concentrated on Australian players, former chairman of the NSW and Australian Rugby League Ken Arthurson commented on how past players such as Bumper Farrell and Ray Stehr would fare today: "If certain that if [Bumper] played in the same manner today he wouldn't appear in too many games – the judiciary would make sure of that. As the game has changed the enforcers have had to clean up their act. The traditional 'softening up' period, highlighted by the odd punch-up, has gone, as have the cheap shots and square-ups. But I'm not suggesting Bumper Farrell or Ray Stehr wouldn't have survived in the current climate. They were great competitors who would have adapted to the times. They could cut it in any company." The same point could be made about Jim – his footballing ability, speed and strength would have been a great asset to any team in the modern game.

It is important to see any sportsman's career in the context of the era in which they played, and Jim's disciplinary record should be examined in this way. In Jim's era, there were contested scrums, a great opportunity for scores to be settled and teams to try to establish domination over the other team's pack. It was accepted that teams had at least one 'enforcer' among its forwards. Fights between the packs, and sometimes more players, were common; although brawls have not been completely eliminated from todays' professional rugby league. High tackles were common, and at least one prominent small international half-back was forced to retire through continually breaking his jaw. It is said, mythically, that in those days, a 'high tackle' was one that missed – i.e. went over the opponent's head. Also, there were no 'sin bins', which were introduced in the 1983–84 season, and can be used today to allow a player to 'cool off', if their coach has not already substituted them if he felt they were in danger of being sent off.

In Jim's era, the game was played by part-time professionals. Winning money could be up to 10 times bigger than losing money. For working class players this was a huge incentive to win, if not by any means possible, certainly at times close to it.

It was after Jim retired that attempts were made to clean up the game. In Australia, from 1980 lengthy bans were handed down as rugby league attempted to change its image, and reduce the level and extent of violence in the game. The ARL felt that this was necessary because the game's image was discouraging younger players from playing it. In 1983, the RFL started a campaign to reduce violence in the game. This was combined with a more regimented approach to the game, which saw it as a sin to concede an unnecessary penalty, let alone to have to play part of the game with only 12 men. In Great Britain, the 1982 and 1986 Australian tourists were a great influence on changing the approach to the game, with a more structured game, greater discipline and less gratuitous violence, even though both squads included players who had very tough reputations.

Even before full-time professionalism at the top level, Collins comments that "By the 1990s, the use of the fist, the arm or the elbow to intimidate an opponent has been replaced to a great extent by a focus on increasing the severity of the tackle." Of Jim's era, he says:

"Up until the 1970s, when the six-tackle rule and the gradual erosion of the importance of scrums reduced the opportunities for violent behaviour, matches often began with a 'softening-up' period, in which the opposing forwards would seek to establish domination through fair means or foul. This was seen as an accepted part of the game by referees as well as players."

Of all the major international football codes, (we cannot comment on Aussie Rules or Gaelic Football), it can be argued that rugby league is the most demanding and physically intensive. It does not have the continual substitutions and players wearing padding and helmets of American Football, or the natural breaks of rugby union. And the physical contact involved in association football, while more intense than is apparent on television, is nowhere near that of rugby league.

Even today, when some older supporters believe that the game is not as 'hard' as it used to be, they would say shown by the shoulder charge being made illegal, a move Jim opposed, the physical demands on the players are tremendous. To establish a strong physical presence by legal means early in the game is still important. And violence – albeit controlled violence – has always been a key part of rugby league.

The two Australian books mentioned above, *Hardmen,* as mentioned above, and *Hit Men* by Tony Adams, celebrate this aspect of the game, although to be fair to Andrews, his book also covers acts of physical and mental courage, and includes Matt King, the former London Broncos player who broke his neck playing for the club's Academy side, and has since gone on as a quadriplegic to qualify as a lawyer. An Australian website, the *Era of the Biff,* also uses much of its space to 'celebrate' the game's tough players. Even though much of the site focuses on Australian players, Jim is fourth in the 'Hardman' category; beaten by Les Boyd, who is top, Vince Karalius, and Kurt Sorensen; but is runner-up in the 'Madman' category, again beaten by Boyd.

Supporters expect an element of violence in rugby league. We enjoy the skills of the game, the great passing moves, and wonderful runs by backs; but also appreciate the 'big hits' as tackles are known today, that knock a feared opponent onto his backside. The game is sometimes known as 'chess with muscles'; the 'chess' element on its own would not be a great spectacle, 'muscle' is still, and hopefully always will be, an important part of the sport.

If you meet Jim Mills off the rugby field, you couldn't meet a nicer man. He sometimes even seems a bit guilty when reminiscing about his playing career, although his success on the after-dinner speaking circuit shows that he can talk about the past with a sense of humour. Even in his late 60s, he still has a powerful physical presence, which no doubt came in useful on occasions when he was running nightclubs in Widnes. His disciplinary record has often overshadowed his achievements on the pitch, particularly after 1972, when his game really developed under the influence of Vince Karalius. This is confirmed by Billy Thompson, who was one of the top referees when Jim played, and had a long and distinguished career with the whistle. Interviewed for this book, he said about Jim: "He could play. He could play in today's game, he had the skills. And he was fast." Now retired, and living in Huddersfield, he retains the sense of humour that is essential for any good referee. When told that a book was being written about Jim Mills, he asked whether it would be 'blood stained'.

Concentrating on club rugby league in England, Jim played 306 first team matches (including 10 appearances off the bench). According to research done by Robert Gate, he was sent off 15 times, i.e. around once every 20 matches. However, of those 15, he was found 'not guilty' once (in 1975–76) and twice received two cautions in a match, which counted as a dismissal (once in 1974–75 and once in 1977–78). Disregard those three, and the total becomes 12, or once every 25 games. The actual statistics are as follows:

Season	First team appearances	Sendings-off
1965–66	5	0
1966–67	11+1	0
1967–68	25+1	2
1968–69	19+2	0
1969–70	31	1
1972–73	22	1
1973–74	27+1	1
1974–75	35	2 (one for 2 cautions)
1975–76	20	1 (not guilty)
1976–77	27	2
1977–78	29	3 (one for 2 cautions)
1978–79	34	2
1979–80	11+5	0

Jim's offences (in the disciplinary committee's language), were as follows: (excludes cautions and 'not guilty')

Punching (one 'vicious')	3
Striking	2
Rough tackle (after warning)	1
Fighting	1
Tripping	1
Vicious shoulder charge & kicking	1
Vicious late head tackle	1
Deliberate kicking	1
Vicious blow with elbow	1

For these dismissals, Jim missed 26 matches through suspension, although he was twice given 'sending off sufficient' by the disciplinary committee. He missed a Regal Trophy Final in 1977–78, and was sent off in his first cup final, the BBC2 Television Trophy match in 1972, and in the 1978–79 Players' Trophy Final against Warrington. He was also sent off twice for Wales, both in 1975. For the first, for 'striking' against England he was banned for two matches, and against New Zealand in November 1975, for 'deliberate and vicious stamping' on John Greengrass, he missed eight matches.

Jim is not the biggest offender in British rugby league. John Burke was sent off at least 18 times in a career that paralleled Jim's. He played for Leeds, Keighley, Castleford and Wakefield Trinity, and was in the Trinity team in the 1979 Challenge Cup Final. He retired due to his disciplinary problems. Ironically, he replaced Jim on the 1979 Lions tour. Some of the newspaper coverage of the change compared their disciplinary records!

Jim believes that "For forwards, the game has completely changed. In my day the head-high tackle was almost legal! There were a lot of hard lads about, many were miners, and then there were the Cumbrian forwards. We needed the money, an extra £20 or £30 a week meant a lot to us. It could get nasty; we were fighting for a living and to keep your place in the side.

When I left Wales, I was still learning, I was not experienced; that was the hard part, learning your trade. There was some give and take. You got to know certain players 'watch his elbow' and so on. You knew what to expect from certain players. My first sending off was by Eric Clay. There was a prop, George Goodyear, who played for Doncaster, and was also a wrestler. We played them at Thrum Hall and he had my head in a wrestling hold, a head lock, so I hit him.

Was I an 'enforcer'? Not early on, but I built up a reputation over the years. I had come from rugby union, and took a lot of whacks from the head high tackles in rugby league. I learnt to lift my arms to protect my head. I thought, 'I'm not going to put up with this,' so I started to give some back. So I got a reputation. By the end of my career, it became easier, because my reputation went before me, people didn't have a go at me.

I was always one of the biggest players on the field, so I had to look after myself. I was never knocked out or broke a bone. But I did get injuries.

For Widnes and for Wales, the opposition would always try to injure our best players, so I needed to protect them. Often when I got sent off, it was protecting my team-mates. The smaller players would get belted a lot, playing against the big fellows. I would get drawn into things that weren't directly to do with me, especially in the test matches."

After 1975, and the Greengrass incident, Jim had a reputation that meant teams would try to wind him up: "Teams would want me off the field. I was not just a hard lad; I did damage as a player for Widnes, teams would be happy to sacrifice one of their players to get me off."

On referees, Jim says that: "Some were very good; I had a lot of time for Billy Thompson. But with some referees, I felt they wanted to be able to say 'I sent Jim Mills off'." One sending off, over 40 years ago, still annoys Jim: "Fred Lindop, in the BBC2 Floodlit Trophy Final in December 1972 against Leigh. It was in the first few minutes. I tackled Geoff Fletcher a bit high. Their prop, Paul Grimes, came running in and started hitting me. I was just blocking him, but Lindop sent the two of us off. Incidents like that, no one was hurt and everyone is tense in the first few minutes of a final. If it had been vicious, and someone had been really hurt, I could understand it, but I felt it was a bad decision.

Of course, in those days there was no 'sin bin' or putting decisions 'on report'. I don't think I deserved all those sendings off. When I played there was retribution away from play; all that has stopped with all the television cameras. But I think the coverage today is tremendous, especially on SKY.

Was I a different person on the pitch? Maybe there was a bit of

'Jekyll and Hyde' about me when I played. I had a job to do and had to do it to the best of my ability. There was violence; it was a physical game about strength, and I used physical strength for my side. But it doesn't affect you as a person. I was different off the field to when I was off the field. But I was a professional, when I was playing rugby I always wanted to win."

When asked about how he would get on playing today, Jim commented: "A lot of us would have done well. We had pace, and with full-time training we would have been better players. Today there are better diets and training, and the injuries are much better looked after. It's all more professional. I would be able to adjust, to play to the current rules; it's a different ball game now. But sometimes I think the referees are too quick to give penalties for high tackles. A player's arm hits the chest and goes up, and all of a sudden it's a penalty. There are too many rule changes, especially the shoulder charge change. I believe they are letting the players down, making a simple game complicated."

Jim's disciplinary career is now, 30 years on, the stuff of legend and after-dinner speeches. On the *Era of the Biff* website, there is a story about Jim giving out awards to the Widnes Tigers junior players in 2006, and being asked why he was sent off so often. The story says that Jim said that two were justified and the rest were 'mistaken identity'. However, the story also says that he was 'great with the kids' and was 'a real gent'.

One of Jim's problems, as outlined above, particularly in the latter half of his career, was that he got the reputation that he could easily be wound up, and, as inevitably happens, the retaliator is the player sent off. Other teams certainly were aware of this. On *YouTube* there is a lovely clip of Jim being interviewed by a young Richard Duckenfield, towards the end of Jim's career, and saying that he 'has been advised to count to three, but doesn't always make it past two...' Certainly, the infamous incident in January 1978 in the Widnes versus Wigan match reflects this short fuse. Wigan's coach was Vince Karalius, who knew Jim well, and had instructed Bill Ashurst to wind Jim up so that he would retaliate and get sent off. The plan worked, within 15 minutes Jim was heading back to the dressing room, sent off for 'vicious punching' according to the official report. However, Ashurst was being carried off, unconscious on a stretcher. One account of this incident says that the punch was wasted; Ashurst was already unconscious from a head-butt. Widnes hung on to win with 12 men, so Karalius's plan was unsuccessful; and Ashurst complained of a headache for some days afterwards. Legend also has it that he said that Karalius could get someone else to wind Jim up next time.

In the Richard Duckenfield interview, Jim points out that he is 17 stone and 'should take a bit of stopping for my size' and it would take a couple of the opposition's forwards to do this.

Jim's propensity to get wound up is confirmed by Billy Thompson: "He never argued with the referees. I would tell him off if I had to. I only sent him off once. But other players would wind him up. He was hard and he got stuck in. He never took a backward step, no one hit him without getting one back, but he was never a problem to referee. He wasn't a dirty player; also he didn't hold grudges and would have a drink with the other team afterwards. Off the field, you couldn't find a better bloke, he was a 'top man', no one could dislike him. Jim would make me laugh at times. I always knew I could control him on the field."

Billy recalls talking to Tom Mitchell when Jim signed for Workington: "Tom said to me 'Look at the size of him.' Mind you, they had a few assassins at that time." Billy remembers sending another player off in a match, and the player complaining to him in the bar after the game: "Jim said to him: 'Have you no sense, don't have a go at the referee, keep quiet.'"

Once, Jim found a way to avoid being sent off. It was when he was playing for Workington at Derwent Park. The referee was Ronnie Campbell, who lived in Widnes. Jim recalls that "Ronnie had asked me for a lift up to Workington. I dropped him outside the ground so no one would see that he had travelled with me. As the game went on, he told me after a rough tackle that he would send me off next time. I told him that if he did he would be walking back to Widnes. Needless to say I did not get sent off." Maybe Jim should have given more referees a lift!

The most serious incident of Jim's career was the 'Greengrass' sending-off at Swansea for Wales against New Zealand on 2 November 1975. Again, the context is important. The match came at the end of a World Championship series where violent play had been an ongoing problem. The format of the tournament, with teams playing each other

131

twice over a calendar year, allowed for grudges to develop and be settled in the return match.

Wales's previous match, against the Australians, had also seen violent play. Part of the background of that was an incident when Jim knocked out Gary Stevens when playing for Great Britain in Australia in the second test in 1974. In his autobiography, Artie Beetson recalls: "During the series, for the first and only time, I kicked an opponent on the football field... there was a huge scrum blow-up in the 14th minute, after the giant Welsh forward Jim Mills necked poor Gary Stevens, our second-rower. He just poleaxed him. It was immediately on, and in the heat of the battle, I kicked Mills, a huge ruthless bloke whose football motto was 'retaliate first', in the ribs. That boot wouldn't have done Mills any harm, but Gary suffered a bad head gash in the blue and returned to the game with his head swathed in bandages. People blamed me for that, but I don't think I was responsible. I do plead guilty, though, to laying the boot on Big Jim." It has to be said that Artie Beetson was a tremendous skilful player, but hardly a shrinking violet on the pitch. Malcolm Andrews says of the Welsh encounter with the Australians in Swansea: "... he [Beetson] led from the front – especially when it came to taming the rough, tough Welshmen ... in the inevitable brawl that spilled over the side-line and into the crowd, Beetson never took a backward step."

The *Rugby Leaguer* reported the incident in the New Zealand match as follows: "The game itself was marred by several ugly incidents, one of which resulted in Jim Mills (Widnes) marching for an early bath. Two minutes from the end, Kiwi prop John Greengrass dived over for a try and Mills appeared to stamp on the player's head. Greengrass needed several stitches in three separate cuts, and Mills – who was cleared last week of allegedly hitting an Oldham player – faces his second disciplinary hearing inside a week. He misses tomorrow's game.

New Zealand full-back Warren Collicoat (cut eye) and stand-off Bob Jarvis (concussion) were also taken off by the New Zealanders. Wales, too, had their victims of the bruising battle. Hooker Tony Fisher went to hospital with a suspected broken arm, stand-off Bill Francis has a compound fracture of the cheek bone and Dave Willicombe damaged his wrist."

This sending-off caused problems for Jim for the rest of his career. He was banned until 1 January 1976, but New Zealand made it clear that he was not welcome to play in their country. This was an issue before the 1977 Lions tour, from which Jim had to withdraw because of injury, and in 1979, when the issue again did not come to a head when Jim had to come home early with a bad knee.

It is to both men's credit that they met up in 2008, and agreed to put the past behind them. Mike Nicholas recalls: "Years later, I was involved in the rapprochement between Jim and John Greengrass. I helped arrange their meeting, and got the *Daily Mail* involved. I thought John Greengrass was a real gentleman, a wonderful guy. I think he'd had enough of the footage of that incident being shown every time there was an incident in a match in New Zealand."

The *Daily Mail* reported that Jim said about their meeting: "I really appreciate it because that incident has niggled me all my rugby career. I didn't just upset John and New Zealand; I upset a lot of people. You couldn't get a worse incident and to have him come over here and offer the hand of friendship means a lot. It's made me feel a lot better. It takes a big man to do what John has done, and I have nothing but the greatest respect for him. I will be eternally sorry for the incident. I only wish that I could turn the clock back."

Jim and Ruth with Chris and John Greengrass.

Billy Thompson – Jim's favourite referee. (Courtesy *Rugby League Journal*)

Greengrass said: "Back home it's brought up all the time. They talk about the worst incidents in football and that's always shown. I was bitter for a couple of years but its water under the bridge. Life's too short to hold grudges. I'd be very disappointed if I'd come all this way and hadn't met Jim." Jim added: "I've only seen the incident once and I cringed. I can't explain it; brainstorm, stupidity, moment of madness. The only thing I can think of is I blamed myself for him scoring."

Jim recalls that "During his stay I took John to have a drink with a lot of the Welsh players from 1975, and they all enjoyed meeting him." Before this match, the question of Jim's temperament, and whether referees were picking on him, had been debated earlier in the year in the *Rugby Leaguer*. Bob Myers, previewing the John Player Trophy final in January 1975, wrote: "Up front, big Jim Mills is running like a tank these days, and given that he can curb his impetuosity, will be a major weapon in attack..."

A few weeks later, on 12 March, the paper had a headline: MILLS

BEING 'GOT AT', and outlined: "Widnes prop Jim Mills may quit the game at the end of the season – because he feels he is being victimised by certain rugby league referees. Matters came to a head for 'Big Jim', a Welsh international, when he was dismissed during the recent England - Wales match at Salford, following an incident with England forward Mike Coulman. 'I've been given the bad boy image, which I don't deserve', he said. 'Some coaches are telling their players to get me off. Referees are penalising me because of my physical strength.'"

The preview of the Challenge Cup Final said on the front page: "'Come and get me' says Mills". The story said: "They're taking bets down Warrington way that Widnes's fiery 17-stone Welsh prop Jim Mills will be the next player to be sent off at Wembley on Saturday. And Wires boss Alex Murphy predicts: 'If Mills isn't sent off, he'll not finish the game anyhow. He'll run out of steam – and that'll suit us.' But big Jim Mills says Wires can forget all thoughts that he can be provoked into taking that long walk. 'I've no intention of getting sent off' he says. 'It doesn't worry me if Wires make me the No.1 target. I'm used to it. In Australia I had 13 men after me every game. I hope Warrington do try to single me out. It makes me play better – and while they're watching me, the rest of our lads will get on with winning the game.'"

Jim scored the try in the match that secured Widnes's win, and did not get sent off. A letter from Glyn Jones of Widnes argued on Jim's behalf: "All too often in the past has Jim been warned or even sent off as a result of retaliation against persistent, niggly tactics employed by opponents in important games to get him dismissed. Examples of this were seen against Leigh (February 1974) and against Rochdale (September 1974). Pity must be felt for a player of his size, who is easily noticed in controversial situations... He is exploited by opposing crowds – remember Leeds versus Widnes last November? – for what are often perfectly legal tackles and badly positioned referees who do not see these incidents are inclined to caution him for something he just hasn't done. For me and thousands more – not just Widnes supporters – Jim Mills is the best prop forward in the League today..."

There was, sometimes, a lighter side to Jim's tangles with the disciplinary committee. He recalls when given a four match suspension in January 1979: "I believe it was a case of mistaken identity. I was nowhere near the incident, but the referee spoke to his touch judge

135

and said 'Off you go Jim, stiff arm tackle'. I tried to explain, but as usual my reputation preceded me and I was summoned to a hearing at Chapeltown Road in Leeds. I was living in Widnes and travelled to Leeds by train. I was starving because I had missed lunch and waited for over an hour to appear before the committee. It had four club directors and the secretary.

As I waited the caterers came into the room where I was waiting with a huge tray of sandwiches. There was a full fresh salmon and crusty bread with salad on the side and I was famished. I thought, I could murder a piece of bread with a bit of salmon. So listening for any sound of movement from the board room, I removed a bit of salmon and piece of bread and ate it. Then I thought they won't miss a bit more and did it again. It was delicious! 'Come in Jim please' said David Oxley as he ushered me into the meeting.

The committee read me the riot act about the 'stiff arm tackle' and told me that my conduct on the field was unacceptable and I must change my ways. It was pointless explaining the 'blue mist' theory to them so I apologised for troubling them and was told that they would discuss my case later and let me know the result by post. Travelling home I thought that I would get a four match ban. A couple of days later the letter arrived with the committee's findings. The ban was for four games; later I heard that I received two games for the stiff arm and two for eating the salmon!"

12. Chairman of Widnes

Having retired as a player, Jim kept in contact with Widnes. However, he had become involved in his first nightclub, which in practice ruled out any day-to-day involvement in coaching. So after a few years, he became a committee member at Widnes: "When I retired I still went and watched the games. In November 1979 I had got involved with the nightclub. Widnes was still a members club in those days and the committee was elected at the AGM. People were elected for three years, and there were three places up for election each year. Some asked me if I was interested. I couldn't play or coach, so it was a way of putting something back into the club, and I found it interesting. I was first elected on in June 1985.

The committee would discuss the club business, the rugby side, and the general running of the club. We would talk to the coach, who would do a report for us. We met every week for a couple of hours. We discussed any major signings, and the comings and goings of players with the coach. When Vince Karalius had come to Widnes as coach, he had made it clear that he wanted complete control of the playing side, and that had continued after he left – the committee were not involved in team selection. Signing players was a committee decision – we had to decide whether we could afford it.

It was a very successful time for the club. In October 1989 we beat Canberra at Old Trafford, which was a great win. We were murdered in the first half. It was like two separate games, we played better than them in the second half. It was a very good Widnes team, with Jonathan Davies, Kurt Sorensen and Martin Offiah."

One of Jim's best memories from his time on the management side of the game was a trip to South Wales. For years there had been speculation about Jonathan Davies, the Welsh rugby union captain, switching codes. He had even been on a trip to Leeds to talk about signing for them, and been taken to a match at Featherstone. In the bar afterwards, none of the local reporters realised who Harry Jepson's friend 'John' really was. St Helens had also been interested in signing him.

Jim accompanied Widnes coach Doug Laughton to South Wales: "Earlier that year [1989] I had been involved in signing Jonathan. I didn't really know him, but we had heard that he was interested in switching codes, and Doug Laughton spoke to him on the phone. We went down to South Wales, stayed the night with my dad in Barry and went to see Jonathan the following night. He lived in Trimsaran, near Llanelli. It was a little village, and we went when it was dark so we weren't seen. His wife Karen invited us in, and made us a cup of tea and a sandwich. Doug did most of the talking, but Jonathan said to me 'How do you think I'll go up there?' I replied that he was a 'great rugby player, had pace and would make the grade'. I think it was to reassure him, and he nodded. We talked to him for about an hour, and he agreed to sign. We arranged to meet at his solicitors in Swansea the next day. We rang the Widnes chairman and agreed the terms.

We went to the car and I said 'I can't believe we've got him, let's have a drink on the way back.' We were still staying at my dad's. We went to John Warlow's pub, but he wasn't there, so we started to drive back to Barry. We were going through Llanelli, and there were lots of pubs, so we stopped at one. There were about six people there, and we ordered a couple of pints. A chap came in who I recognised. He asked us 'Have you come to sign any players?' We said 'No', we'd been to visit John Warlow. The man was Norman Gale, a former Welsh international hooker. There were photos of Llanelli players all over the pub. He bought us a drink and said that his son played for Llanelli. I asked him if he was involved in the club, where Jonathan played, and he said 'Involved? I'm the chairman.' I couldn't believe it, of all the pubs we had to pick... We said we had to go and he came out to give us directions.

We told Jonathan what had happened when we saw him the next day. I could imagine him picking up a newspaper the next day and reading that Jonathan had signed for Widnes. He'd bought us a pint and we'd signed his star player. In 1993 I saw him at Terry Price's funeral. I went up to him and said 'All right?' but he wasn't pleased to see me."

Jim recalls that handling their new signing was very important: "Doug was very shrewd when Jonathan joined the club. He nursed him along, and played him in the 'A' team, which drew a big crowd. He played him off the bench, and gradually settled him in. Jonathan was a very intelligent player, and he soon picked the game up. Doug and I had no doubt that he would be a great player, and he was also a nice lad to have around the club."

In Davies's biography, *Code Breaker*, he says that he had told Doug Laughton on the phone that he did not intend to join Widnes, but Laughton replied that he and Jim Mills would come anyway, so he could say this direct to them. He then asked for "a ridiculously high amount" which Widnes agreed to pay, leaving him to reflect that maybe he hadn't asked for enough! But what is also clear is that Davies was fed up with how he was being treated by the WRU: "I regarded myself as friendless and unappreciated and the only soothing voices belonged to Doug Laughton and Jim Mills. The way they talked about their game impressed me. It appeared that nothing mattered except how good you were. I was desperately uncertain how I would fare in league, but if men of that quality were prepared to place their reputations on the line, why shouldn't I? They gave me more confidence in myself than I ever received from the WRU."

Looking back, Jim says that he was a "gamekeeper turned poacher" – "I had been signed by a rugby league scout, now I was doing the same." Not every trip to Wales was successful: "Doug and I went to Neath to watch a player called Elgin Rees. We went for a pint afterwards in the clubhouse, and one of the Neath officials, a former player, came over and said to Doug 'You have to leave, and take that thug with you' – meaning me. Doug said 'I'll go; you go and tell Jim what you said about him.' He didn't come over, and we shouldn't really have gone in there. They all knew why we were there."

With Jonathan Davies, Frank Myler and Frank Nyland.

Jonathan Davies wasn't the only rugby union player who Widnes signed. Another was a little-known winger from London: "Martin Offiah was another rugby union player that Doug found for us. Doug spoke to the committee before he went to sign him; he had seen him playing for Rosslyn Park. He went down to London, and gave him £1,000 at first. Of course he got more money later. He was a wonderful player, with great pace; it was a shame we had to sell him to Wigan. He was a good mixer, and a nice lad, good for team spirit. We also signed John Devereux and Paul Moriarty from rugby union, and Doug had signed Andy Gregory and Joe Lydon from under Wigan's nose. That was a very good Widnes side. In 1993, we played Wigan in the Challenge Cup Final and should have beaten them. Richie Eyres was sent off, but that wasn't why we lost."

By then, Jim had become club chairman, a post he held for five years: "Ray Owen had been the club chairman for a long time. In 1991 I said I would stand. There was no bad blood between us, and I was voted in by the committee. It's interesting to look back at the people who were on the board and the committee during the time I was involved. Some were former players, such as Ray who had played for the club in the 1964 Challenge Cup Final. Tom Smith, Wilf Hunt and Ged Lowe had also played professionally, and a couple of others had played in the amateur game. The rest were mainly from businesses that had a connection to the town, and brought their experience to the club. Frank Nyland was the club solicitor. Audrey Spencer was the only woman involved in my time. She was very involved with the supporters association.

During my time as chairman the club changed from being a members' club to a limited company. My role was running the business, and working with the other directors. We sold the ground to the local council, and I was involved in at the start of the negotiations over that, along with Frank Nyland and Tom Fleet.

Another part of the job I enjoyed was welcoming the other team's directors to the club. We would have a buffet and I would make a speech to welcome them. I liked doing that, and meeting the characters from different clubs."

One task that fell to Jim was to deal with the departure of one of the club's stars: "I negotiated the sale of Martin Offiah to Wigan for a then world record transfer fee. He had been on the 1991 Lions tour, and when he came back he didn't want to play for us anymore. Maurice Lindsay had been the tour manager. I was in a board meeting, and Maurice phoned to tell me that he had sold Ellery Hanley to Leeds for £250,000. 'I want to give that to you' he said. 'Fine', I replied, 'Send it over'. But he wanted Martin Offiah. Now, Martin was in his pomp at that time, whereas Ellery was coming to the end of his career. I put it to the committee, who said 'No', so I told Maurice he was not for sale.

Now, the committee knew that Martin didn't want to play for us anymore, but we wanted to get as much as we could for him. He had a 10 year contract with us, but if someone doesn't want to play for you, you have to make the best if it. If a player wants to go, you can't hold onto them.

This went on, and the Challenge Cup deadline was coming up. I said that we wanted £500,000; I didn't care what the world record was. Maurice went to £370,000, then £380,000. I said £450,000 – he said that if he put the phone down the deal's off. It was like a game of poker. He put the phone down.

Thirty minutes later he rang again: £430,000. I said split the difference and the deal was done. So we settled on £440,000. It was a world record cash fee at the time, and lasted until Stuart Fielden's transfer to Wigan in 2006. We didn't want to lose him, but we had no option and I got as much for the club as I could."

Despite the loss of Martin Offiah, Widnes won the Regal Trophy that season. Jim recalls that "We beat Leeds 24–0 in the final at Wigan. Frank Myler was our coach."

In 1992, Jim and Sam Evans visited South Africa: "We were invited by Dave Southern, who was working to build the game there. Dave is from Widnes, and we went with two Halifax directors. We took a Widnes kit to give to one of the teams. We watched a couple of matches in Pretoria. There was a good atmosphere. We met Tom van Vollenhoven, and went to see Johnny Gaydon, who used to play for Widnes. It wasn't a scouting trip as such, just to give them some support."

Jim had played in three Challenge Cup Finals, but in 1993 experienced events from the Royal Box rather than the front row of the scrum: "Another great experience as club chairman was the 1993 Challenge Cup Final. Before the game there was a big lunch with all the dignitaries. Neil Kinnock was there, and Michael Parkinson. In the Royal Box was Keith Rowlands, who was president of the Welsh Rugby Union. I had a chat with him – we had played together at Cardiff.

I remember going into the dressing room as chairman, and wishing the team good luck. My experience as a player was useful; I knew what they were facing. During the game I was so focussed that being in the Royal Box didn't make a difference to me. We had a good reception after the game; I made a speech and said that we were just as good as Wigan.

Phil Larder was our coach at Wembley. Frank Myler had stood down, and moved into an office job as football secretary. Phil was a modern coach; he produced a 10 page report on each match. They were too much for me to read, but I never told him because I didn't want to upset him." Part of Jim's role was dealing with the players: "As chairman I did deal with some problems with players, or the negotiations if a player was leaving. Sometimes I would have to sort things out if a player had been dropped. But I was always a players' man, I didn't want to fall out with people."

Super League

In April 1995, the game was torn apart over the proposed 'Super League'. The issues involved have been outlined many times in different books and reports, and it is not necessary to go over them again here. However, it is important to outline the unique – and horrible – experience that Widnes had. The sequence of events is outlined below:

Widnes and Super League

Wednesday 5 April: Rugby League Council scheduled meeting in Leeds. Summer rugby debated. During meeting, Maurice Lindsay takes phone call and outlines to the Council about News Ltd's approach to the game about Super League (SL). He had been in London the day before to meet BskyB after News Ltd's first approach about SL.

Friday 7 April: Hastily arranged meeting at Huddersfield for First Division clubs and Hull KR. Jim Mills (JM) did not attend – was at

Aintree Races and was not contacted. Proposed that Widnes were first reserve for SL.

Saturday 8 April: *Meeting at Wigan of club chairmen proposes SL of 14 clubs including six merged clubs. Widnes in SL, but only through a merger with Warrington.*

Thursday 13 April: *Meeting at Manchester Airport Hilton of club chairmen. Agrees SL of 14 clubs. JM told that one of the French clubs could be going to withdraw and Widnes would take their place.*

Friday 14 April: *(Good Friday): Widnes versus Warrington. JM is phoned by Maurice Lindsay who confirms that one of the French teams has withdrawn from SL and therefore Widnes will be members. JM announces this to the crowd before the match.*

Final SL line-up not to be settled until 4 May, when Rodney Walker and a judge would meet to decide this, once the outcome of potential mergers is known. This was subsequently cancelled.

Sunday 30 April: *Meeting of all club chairmen at Huddersfield decided that top 10 teams in 1994–95 First Division with London and Paris would become the 12 clubs in SL (reduced from 14 clubs). Widnes only club to vote against, Keighley Cougars were not in the meeting.*

Tuesday 2 May: *Widnes start legal proceedings against the RFL after losing their SL place.*

Friday 5 May: *Widnes go to court for an injunction. Case adjourned.*

Widnes then proposed a play-off scheme for 1995–96 season to decide the SL places, but there was little support for this – clubs who were already in SL were not interested.

Wednesday 17 May: *Tom Smith resigns as a Widnes director, because of conflict of interest in the SL dispute with his role as an RFL director.*

Thursday 25 and Friday 26 May: Widnes case for an injunction against the RFL heard at Manchester Crown Court. Judge finds in favour of the RFL.

Monday 5 June: Reported that Widnes will sign the agreement that set up SL, once the club had been given assurances that there would be promotion and relegation from the first season.

Jim was in the front line because Widnes's future as a top level club was at stake: "I was at a meeting at the RFL [5 April], I was the Council member for Widnes. Maurice Lindsay [who by then had become chief executive of the RFL], was called out of the meeting to take a phone call. He came back and told us that 'Sky wanted to "take over the game"', and that the phone call had been from Rupert Murdoch. He wanted us to 'make our minds up', but no decision was taken that day."

Two days later, on 7 April, a crucial meeting was held. Jim outlines: "Soon afterwards, I went to the races at Aintree for the day and was speaking at a dinner in the evening. A meeting was called at short notice, and Tom Smith, the Widnes vice-chairman went because they couldn't get hold of me. I had my mobile phone with me and didn't receive any calls. There were a few other chairman who didn't get there. Anyway, they had the meeting and put the new Super League together, and Widnes were the first reserve. I got hold of Maurice Lindsay and complained that there had been no notice given of the meeting; there was a big fall out."

One of the aspects of the Super League proposals that most upset the fans were that longstanding local rivals should merge to form 'super-clubs'. Simon Kelner, in his book *To Jerusalem and Back*, outlines: "Mills made an impassioned speech [on 8 April] about the traditions of his club and their record of success, which over the past two decades had been better only by Wigan. He received much support from the floor." He quotes Jim as saying: "I played hell with them. A lot of them sat there with their mouths open. I couldn't believe we were expected to make decisions about the future of the game with such little notice. I felt that the negotiations were done much too quickly, and too few people were involved. There was a definite feeling that everything had to be done today, or the money would disappear tomorrow." Despite Jim's forceful arguments, Malcolm White, the

144

chairman of Swinton, proposed that Warrington and Widnes merge.

Fans from all areas of the game were horrified at what seemed to be happening to their sport, and a group of them quickly published a booklet, *Merging on the Ridiculous*, in response to the merger plans in particular. There was only one contribution from a Widnes fan, who wrote: "Had the loyal followers of this great club really been put through three years of team decimation, the desperate measure of 'Widnes in Need' and the share offer and the sale of our ground to get into the black, just for the RFL to decide we were no longer viable?"

On Wednesday 12 April, the front page of the *Widnes Weekly News* had a banner headline: "KICK MERGER INTO TOUCH". Sports editor Dave Bettley's report outlined: "Shocked Widnes RLFC fans are putting up a united front to save the town's club from a merger with arch-rivals Warrington. Furious fans vowed to fight moves to amalgamate Widnes with Warrington as part of a revolutionary new summer Super League. Naughton Park directors were in emergency session last night to discuss the proposed merger under the banner of Cheshire.

Chairman Jim Mills is in favour of a Super League and believes Widnes must be part of it. But, as former World Club champions and one of the most successful teams in the last 20 years, he argued Widnes should be members in their own right.

The new 14-team competition was given the go-ahead in just 96 hours after an approach by representatives of media magnate Rupert Murdoch whose Sky TV company will cover games.

'We are about to embark with the council on building a new stadium' said Mr Mills. 'With the influx of money which will allow us to buy new players, we're quite capable of competing with anybody next season in a top class stadium which will be second to none.'"

The report continued: "Widnes Supporters Club chairman Alan Rae said of the merger proposals: 'This stinks. It's a complete disgrace. Widnes is a big name in rugby league and the supporters feel that we have been sold down the river.'"

The paper's sports pages covered the story in more detail, in a report headed 'Overnight mistake': "Widnes have blasted a decision to omit them from the original Super League... Only intervention from Mr Mills at a meeting in Wigan on Saturday saved Widnes from being left with the minnows in a new First Division." It reports Jim as saying: "I put our case and said it was a disgrace they had come to a decision without the chairman of the club being there. I wanted to know why Warrington were allowed to go on their own and us not be considered. I asked what criteria the decision was made on. If you look at the gates for the last 10 years, we have averaged a thousand more than Warrington. I said one of the most successful clubs in rugby league over 20 years had been cast aside and Second Division clubs put in the Super League. A lot of the club chairmen supported what I said. The decision was right to go into this new Super League because if you look outside Wigan and Leeds, the game is in financial trouble. Where they made the mistake was trying to put the structure together overnight."

The report said out that "Both Widnes and Warrington are planning new stadiums, but Mr Mills added: 'It's obvious it would be more advantageous for them to come to Widnes than us go to Warrington. Our stadium is about to be built and Warrington's stadium isn't even in the decision stage and they haven't got any land to build it on.'"

The move towards mergers eventually collapsed, but at   enormous cost to Widnes: "There were lots of arguments, and it all came to a head. Maurice Lindsay organised a meeting at the Hilton Hotel at Manchester Airport on 13 April. The day before, Peter Higham, the Warrington chairman rang me. He said that Maurice had asked me to ring him to say don't put any pressure on Maurice at the   meeting because one of the French teams were going to pull out of Super League and Widnes would be in, but he could not divulge this at the meeting, so I agreed to play along. There was a delegation from Keighley, but their application to join was rejected. I felt that in all the discussions on Super League, people looked after their own interests, and didn't look at things for the benefit of the game.

I kept quiet in the meeting, and spoke to Maurice after the meeting, and told him not to let me down. He said that he would ring me the next day [Good Friday 14 April], when we were playing Warrington, after he had the meeting with the French team. If it was good news I could announce it to the crowd.

Maurice did ring me, before the game had started, and told me that the French team had pulled out. I announced this to the crowd, and everyone from both teams was excited. Two weeks later, we were thrown out again, and I feel that I was conned. How can you work with people like this?"

After the Warrington game, the *Widnes Weekly News's* front page headline was "JUBILATION". The paper reported that 97 per cent of readers in a telephone poll had been against the merger. The report said that Jim had told the crowd at the match: "It's wonderful news. We start building for the future tomorrow."

Alan Rae commented that: "Jim Mills did magnificently. For three years he's been chairman, he's had nothing but trouble and you can only admire him." Widnes supporter Chris Whitfield recalls both sets of supporters having a peaceful demo on the pitch at half-time, and "Jim Mills addressed the fans and stated that he had been informed that both clubs had been admitted to Super League on their own merit. Both sets of fans applauded the decision, but as we all know that decision was changed and teams that had one good season (Oldham, Workington) and a French team (Paris) were admitted instead of ourselves. That decision has irked Widnes fans since Super League started and that feeling of utter disbelief re-emerged years later when Salford and Celtic Crusaders were given a franchise ahead of Widnes."

Widnes supporter Phil Fearnley recalls that "Widnes's recent record demanded more respect; all teams go through periods of transition... On reflection, Widnes were caught up in a global media war at a time when the club were going through a period of change. Don't forget Halifax were one of the five in the original SL plan who didn't have to merge. Look at them now; they got into a terrible financial mess." Fearnley also says that Jim was not blamed for the mess, but that "most invective was aimed at Maurice Lindsay".

Looking back, Jim believes that "It was wrong to bring in a new system without a season to decide who's going to play where. They changed the rules at the end of the season. We'd had our worst season for ages, we had a lot of injuries, and that took us down the league. We had been one of the most successful clubs in the game, had been World Club Champions, and had brought players such as Jonathan Davies and Martin Offiah into the game. We had recognised the need to improve our income, and cut expenditure, in line with the *Framing the Future* document the RFL had produced. We had got rid of some experienced players. We weren't to know that the final table of that season would determine the composition of Super League. We were trying to get our club in order financially."

Kelner outlines that in the final meeting, with Keighley refusing to be in the room, only Widnes voted against: "Only Widnes, who had ridden an emotional switchback – first excluded, then told to merge, then included, and finally, because of their league position, left out again – voted against the new plan and resolved to institute a legal action of their own." He continues: "Jim Mills, the Widnes chairman, then raised the temperature of the meeting by suggesting that 'some people had been less than 100 per cent truthful.'" This provoked an impassioned defence of Maurice Lindsay by Rodney Walker.

The *Widnes Weekly News* reported that Jim was warned in advance of what the outcome of the meeting could be. A report by Dave Bettley headed "Mills fury at 'farce'" outlined: "...Naughton Park chairman Jim Mills admitted he had seen it coming. All speculation pointed to the Super League being expanded. But instead, the number of clubs in the new premier division was cut by two at a meeting of club chairman in Huddersfield on Sunday... Widnes club director Tom Smith, also a member of the RL board, had told him last Friday what might happen.

... The Naughton Park chairman said: 'We are the only team who were definitely in the Super League and are not in it today because all the other clubs were there through mergers [in the original Super League proposals]. The way they have gone about putting it together has been an absolute farce. A couple of kids could have organised it better.

I think it is a disgrace how they have treated a club like Widnes. We are the second most successful club in the Rugby League. We are the only British club apart from Wigan who have been World Champions.'

With this season's top 10 First Division clubs being allocated a Super League place, Widnes are paying the price for a run of seven defeats at the end of the season. But Mr Mills says injuries rather than complacency were to blame: 'Even so, we didn't get relegated' he added, 'But overnight and just on another whim, they have put us in what is a Second Division. Our record in rugby league should be acknowledged. It's so short-sighted just to look at this season, when we have been putting our house in order. There are clubs who have managed to get into the Super League who are millions of pounds in debt. We are being penalised while clubs who have spent money they haven't got are benefitting by it.'"

Jim recalls: "We took the RFL to court; I thought we had a chance of winning, but they had very good lawyers. The judge said that all the other clubs had agreed to the new structure. It was just the lawyers arguing in court, I didn't have to give evidence.

Once we were out of Super League, players wanted to leave because they wanted to play in Super League. It decimated the club. One of the most successful clubs was thrown out of the elite. We were also negotiating for the new ground at the time, and that decision had an effect on that as well."

The court case was heard at Manchester Crown Court on 25 and 26 May 1995, in front of Justice Parker. John Martin QC appeared for Widnes and Michael Beloff QC – one of the top 20 QCs in the country – for the RFL. After the legal submissions from both sides, the judge rejected Widnes's arguments. Part of his judgement was that as chief executive, Maurice Lindsay was there to implement the board's decisions, and that Widnes should not have accepted his statement as the RFL's decision when he phoned Jim during the match at Warrington. Tom Smith, the Widnes vice-chairman, was a member of the RFL board, and had agreed to the original decision. Doubtless he was under a lot of pressure, but that did not help Widnes's case.

It is interesting to examine – with the benefit of hindsight – what happened to the 12 clubs chosen for the first season of Super League. As Chris Whitfield points out, Workington struggled and were relegated after the first season; and the Oldham Bears and Paris St Germain only lasted two seasons. The 'Bears' reformed as a 'new' club in Oldham; Paris disappeared after failing to build on a successful first season; although France is now well represented by the Catalan Dragons. Halifax and Sheffield Eagles are now playing in the Championship; the Eagles having been reformed after a 'shotgun wedding' style merger with the Huddersfield Giants in 1999. Only six of the original clubs have been members of Super League for every season since then, and three of them have survived major financial problems.

As Jim feared, some of the club's top players left Widnes. In June 1996, David and Paul Hulme joined Leeds and Warrington respectively, and Emosi Koloto and Karle Hammond also moved on to pastures new. Widnes used 35 players in the first team in 1996, and only finished seventh out of 11 clubs in the new 'First Division'. It took years for the club to recover from not being admitted into the initial Super League. Today, Jim says that "It is great to see Widnes back in Super League where they belong, but I still believe it was a big mistake to leave them out from day one, and when you look what happened to the original SL clubs, it proves that those responsible did rugby league no favours."

149

Left: With Frank Myler at Naughton Park in November 1996, when the rebuilding was starting. (Photo: Darrell Cooper)
Below: Widnes 1996, with Jim as chairman and Doug Laughton as coach. (Photo: Aaron Photography)

Looking back, Jim reflects: "After my experience with Super League, I was fed up. We were also involved with the detailed negotiations about the new ground. Tony Chambers was involved with the negotiations as well, and he was a director of P&O Properties. I felt that he could take the club forward, and he was happy to take over, so I told the committee. He was a good chairman. We sold some shares to bring in some more capital to the club. I stayed on the board for a few years. The main thing was to get the new ground up and running.

I came off the board in October 2005. By then we had bought a second nightclub, so I had two clubs to run. I would get home at 3 or 4 in the morning. I was too tired and I couldn't get to the games."

Jim still follows the club: "My business partner Sam Evans has an executive box at Widnes and we go as often as possible, and I watch on television as well. I go and watch David play occasionally. I watched him in Super League, especially for Widnes."

13. A nightclub in Widnes

For most of his rugby league career, Jim saw rugby league as his main job, even though he was playing part-time. But from 1979 until a couple of years ago, he was involved in the nightclub business: "I had a lot of different jobs before getting involved in the nightclub business. In reality, rugby league was my main job. The extra money from working and playing was good. When I came to Widnes the chairman, Jim Davies, got me a job with Bass Charrington. I could get time off for rugby, they would let me go on tour and then come back. The Widnes team did a tour of the brewery once; there were a lot of headaches after that.

Another job I had was doing some labouring on a building site. I got talking to another chap when we were having a break, and it turned out to be Maurice Colclough, who played rugby union for England. He played for Liverpool St Helens.

I was coming to the end of my career. After a game, I went to the Wheel club in Widnes with Sammy Evans. He was a Widnes supporter and good friend of mine who ran a scrapyard. There were only two nightclubs in Widnes at the time. We were at the bar, and the place was dismal. It was a big building as well.

I said to Sammy 'There are no decent clubs in Widnes. We could buy this place and do it up.' So we had a word with the owner, and asked if he was interested in selling. 'Make me an offer' he said. His name was Steve Bond, and he owned a taxi firm at the time. We went to his house, agreed a fee and Sammy and I bought it, 50/50.

We spent a lot of money on doing the place up, some of which we borrowed from the brewery. Sammy was very 'hands-on doing the work on the club. I was clerk of works; he said I was lazy and never got my hands dirty! It became 'Big Jim's'. We put in a big dance floor, we could have a disco, or cabaret acts. There was a well-known local group, the Houghton Weavers, who used to play there. And we had comedians, people like Bernard Manning. He became a good friend; we went to his 70th birthday do in Manchester. A lot of the people from Coronation Street were there, and Neil and Christine Hamilton. He used to invite us to his Embassy club in Manchester as well. Emlyn Hughes and Ian Rush used to come in. We had a link with Liverpool FC because we used to get treatment from a physio there, who Frank Myler knew."

151

The club was soon very successful: "It was packed, seven days a week, for years. There was still the other club, the Landmark, at the other end of town. We bought that as well. I ran the nightclubs and Sammy continued to develop his scrap and demolition business, which he still runs. Over the years Sammy has built up a huge demolition and scrap metal business. He is now a wealthy man, but thrives on hard work and deserves his success.

I used to employ all the staff, book the acts and order the drinks. We had a manager in the other club, and had a steak bar there at one time.

Opening Big Jim's nightclub.

I enjoyed the work, but it was very tiring, seven days a week, getting home at three o'clock in the morning.

In the early years, there were a few problems with local idiots, and a few punch-ups. Some lads, if we didn't let them in, would become a problem. My reputation as a rugby league player was never an issue though. In fact, it helped that the rugby league players would come to the club; and that helped the business. Once we had the Welsh rugby union team there, and players from other rugby league clubs would call in as well"

Inevitably with such a business, there could be problems: "I once got a phone call from someone with a Liverpool accent saying that we 'needed protection'. 'Why don't you come to the club and I'll show you who needs protection' I replied. I never heard from him again and we never had to pay for protection. Sometimes there were complaints from the neighbours, and we would have to go to court to keep our licence.

After 15 years we did the club up, and changed the name. It

152

became the 'Top of the Town'. We changed the Landmark as well. The upstairs became Sam's nightclub; while on the ground floor we had an *a la carte* restaurant. That didn't do very well, so we changed it to Frenchy's Wine Bar, which was more successful.

Widnes player Kurt Sorensen got involved. I wanted to move on, so we sold a part-share to him. He was involved for about four years, but then he wanted to go back to Australia, so we bought him out. I'm still in contact with him. I made a good living from the nightclubs, but it was hard work. One problem that developed during the last few years was drugs, and people bringing drugs in. There were also more problems after closing time."

Jim also recalls a couple of lads making trouble in the club, and fighting. One was thrown out of the front entrance, the other through the back, hoping that they would go their separate ways. But they continued their confrontation out the front, until the doormen went out to stop the incident. One ran off, the other was left lying in the road with a head wound, and Jim had to call an ambulance.

Once, Jim didn't even get in the door: "I'd put my suit on at home and driven in to the club. As I got there the doormen had just thrown someone out. He was kicking the door of the club when I arrived. I said 'What do you want?' he said: 'To go in'. I said no, and he grabbed my shirt and threw a punch at me. To get him off me I flattened him, but he had torn my shirt, and I had to go home and get changed."

On another occasion, things got more serious. A local 'heavy' was causing problems and was asked to leave. Jim had gone over to the door to see what the problem was. The man left reluctantly, with his girlfriend, got into his car and started driving up and down within inches of Jim's Mercedes, which was parked on the other side of the street. Jim went out of the club to see what was happening, and the 'heavy' then started ramming the back of Jim's car. Jim managed to stop him, and after a confrontation, the man left. However, he went straight to the local police station to complain about Jim. An inspector rang Jim at the club, and asked him to come down to the station to give his side of the story. When he got there he saw the 'heavy' who was well-known to the police, still bleeding from the incident.

Jim explained what happened; no further action was taken. The man was never seen again at the club. Jim thinks that many people were pleased that a local bully had got a taste of his own medicine!

A night at Big Jim's: Glyn Shaw, Peter Holland, Jim, Bob Blackwood

However, gradually the business declined: "Changes in the licensing laws meant that there were more late bars around. We cut back to two or three nights a week, and then closed the business down; although we still own the building. We had run the club for 30 years; a lot of people have good memories from it, and had met their husbands or wives there."

One other activity that Jim enjoys, although just for charity, is after-dinner speaking. He speaks at five or six dinners a year, and often takes Billy Boston with him as a special guest.

Billy was coming towards the end of his career with Wigan as Jim was establishing himself in rugby league. However, the two meet regularly, and for this book Billy wrote that: "Jim Mills is a Welshman notorious by reputation, a hard man, but most of all a talented rugby union and British Lion rugby league player. No doubt this book will tell many tales of his notoriety both in the UK and down under. I never played against Jim so have no scars to show. To me Jim Mills is a kind hearted, honest guy that I am proud to call one of my best friends."

In 2011, Jim spoke at a rugby union dinner in Llanelli. At one time, he was a feared figure among club officials, who if they saw him at a match would worry about which of their star players was being targeted to join Widnes. Now, he is a welcome guest speaker at their dinners. On this occasion, Jim donated half his fee to the Swansea Valley Miners Appeal Fund; which was raising money for the families of four miners who had died in a mining accident. A letter from Peter Hain, the MP for Neath, thanked Jim for his support. Llanelli former players chairman, British Lions and Wales international Terry Davies commented that they were very honoured to have Jim speaking at the dinner, and "it is the mark of the man that he is helping the miners while returning to South Wales." Jim has also been the guest speaker at the Cardiff Past Players Association, and is always welcome at their functions.

Jim has established a good reputation on the after-dinner speaking circuit in both codes. Huddersfield RUFC president Paul Giblin wrote to him in February 2013 to say that "It was a great night and a lot of fun and I am pleased to see that you are still able to 'stamp your authority'. It was a pleasure to meet yourself and Billy and you certainly gave us a lot to talk about."

The two rugby codes meet on the cruise ship Oriana.
From left: Scott Hastings, Jim, Gareth Edwards and Willie John McBride.

A dinner with Garfield Owen in Halifax in 1998. Standing: Jack Scroby, not known, Billy Boston, Alan Kellet, Kel Coslett, Jim; sitting: Lewis Jones, Clive Rowlands, Les Pearce, Garfield Owen and Geoff Pimblett.

Top: Ruth and Jim on holiday in Spain.

Middle: Jim with his hero, Bryn Terfel, the Welsh opera singer, on holiday in Spain.

Right: Ruth and her horse Bonny.

Two prop forwards: David and Jim in David's early days at Widnes.

Meeting old friends at the North Sydney Leagues Club in 1979.
From left: John Grey, Harry McKinnon, Jim, Doug Laughton and Harry Forbes (North Sydney secretary).

14. Family life

Jim still has relatives and friends in South Wales; however his mother died in 1987 at the age of 70. His father lived in Barry until he died at the age of 82 in 2000. Jim had a brother, David, who was tragically killed in a road accident in 1972 at the age of 30, when Jim was playing for North Sydney. Jim and Doug Laughton stayed with Jim's father in Barry when they made their famous trip to sign Jonathan Davies from Llanelli in 1989.

While living in Halifax, Jim met Angela Gabbitas, who was the cousin of the Hunslet and Great Britain stand-off, Brian Gabbitas. They were married in 1966 and Colin Dixon was Jim's best man. The couple had two children, Gareth, who was born on 4 October 1966, and Julie who was born on 11 April 1968. However, the marriage broke up, and the couple subsequently divorced. Gareth later married a Maltese girl, Helen, and lived for some years in Malta, but is now back in Halifax. Jim sees him regularly.

Julie tragically died of breast cancer, aged only 30, in February 1999. She had built up a good business as a beautician in Rawson Street in Halifax called the Beauty Mill, which had a very good reputation. Jim set up the Julie Mills Fund, as part of the Widnes and Runcorn Cancer Support Group in her memory. Most of his fees for after-dinner speaking are donated to this charity. A letter he received from Dee Graal, the group's co-ordinator, in August 2012, thanked him for a donation of £350, and said "It really is wonderful how you always remember us when donating your fees. The 'Julie Mills Fund' continues to provide cards, flowers and subsidised outings for our Bosom Buddies members and we are now planning our annual party..."

Jim and Ruth met when they were both working at Bass Charrington. She moved in with him on 18 March 1980; coincidentally the day Jim was injured playing against Bradford Northern for Widnes. This injury finished his career, so she never saw him play live. Doug Laughton brought him home after the match, he was then in hospital for a week and in plaster for six weeks. Ruth ruefully recalls "I was his nurse, I thought when I moved in I'd be sinking in his arms, but ended up, up to my arms in his sink!"

Left: Jim's daughter Julie at her shop, the Beauty Mill, in Rawson Street, Halifax.

Right: Jim, his son Gareth and uncle Gordon in Halifax.

Ruth and Jim with Gareth, his wife Helen and auntie Hilda,
Enjoying a pub meal near Halifax.

160

Their son David was born on 1 June 1981 and their daughter Katie on 24 June 1983. Jim and Ruth got married at Northwich Registry office on 19 September 1985. Jim`s best man was his mate Doug Laughton.

The family have lived in Frodsham for many years, and moved into their current home in 1988. Ruth had horses at the time and the house came with a field next to it and a big garden. They built a stable block at the bottom of the garden, and at one time had three horses. Ruth recalls it was very hard work looking after the horses, and now they don`t have horses any more, she spends much of her time looking after the large garden.

Katie

Ruth gave up work when she had the children. The couple now have four grandchildren. David and his partner Julia have two boys, Tyler and Sonny; while Katie and her partner Craig have Finlay and Rohan.

Ruth and Jim have an apartment in Spain and enjoy taking their grandchildren there, Jim says that "Ruth is good with the kids" while Ruth was pleased when one of them said to her recently," I love your house by the sea Nannie".

David says that Jim "is a great family man. I've got two kids, and my sister has two. He's great with them, a big teddy bear. All his grandchildren love him to bits. And he was a good dad to me when I was young."

Jim and Ruth have been together for 33 years and are clearly very happy. One area Ruth tries to have some influence, not always with success, is Jim`s diet, although he looks very fit. Some of the interviews for this book took place in the kitchen of their house in Frodsham.

When we stopped for lunch in one of them, Jim suddenly looked a bit mournful: "Peter, she`s got me on a diet; its salad for lunch". Out of the fridge came two enormous plates of salad that Ruth had prepared before going out, one of which certainly fed the writer very well. But next time we were back to ham sandwiches and pies, so the new regime didn't last long.

Jim and Ruth with the family: Adults: Julia and David, Ruth and Jim, Craig and Kate; children: Tyler and Sonny, Rohan and Finlay.

Jim and Ruth with the grandchildren. Ruth holding Sonny, Jim holding Rohan, Tyler and Finlay standing.
(Both photos: Darren Crawley)

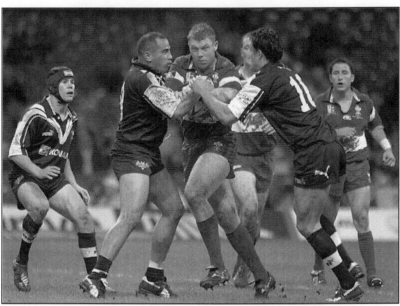

David in action for Wales against New Zealand.
(Photos: David Williams – rlphotos.com)

163

Katie works in a Chester hair salon as a senior stylist. In her spare time she likes to keep fit by running. She has run in several races including the Chester half marathon to raise money for the Alder Hey Children's Hospital. She also runs in organised 10k runs over the North West and participates in Race for Life every year. Jim and Ruth are very proud of her achievements.

David followed in Jim`s footsteps and became a full-time rugby league player in the front row. He has played Super League first team football for Widnes, Hull Kingston Rovers and Harlequins RL and of course Wales, including captaining the Welsh side. David has also played for Leigh and is currently playing at Swinton.

While David was playing at Hull KR, Ruth and Jim discovered one of the problems of having a son who plays professional rugby league. At 6am one morning, the doorbell rang; bleary eyed Jim answered the door. It was the RFL's drug-testers, doing a random check on David. Jim recalls: "I told them he was living in Hull, but they still sat outside for two hours in case he turned up." Apparently David got told off because he had not given the RFL his new address.

Ruth had little knowledge of rugby league before she met Jim, but did enjoy going to the matches when he was Chairman of Widnes. She recalls running on the pitch at Central Park when Widnes won the Regal Trophy in 1992; much to the horror of Maurice Lindsay, then the Wigan chairman.

She encouraged David to play when he was young, and use to take him to matches. David has played the game in a very different era from Jim, and while Jim was clearly pleased that David took up the game, he stayed in the background, and probably helped David's development by putting less pressure on him. David says that "When I first started out, Jim never pushed me to get involved. It was a friend who first took me to a local club. In fact, it was my mum who drove me to the matches and training. It was a big commitment on her part, when I played in Widnes and then joined St Helens Crusaders. I think in the early days Jim didn't want to be seen as putting pressure on me." Interviewed by Andy Wilson for *Rugby League World* in 2002, when he was playing for Widnes, David said that he was "very aware of everything his dad did... I've been watching videos since I was young... and I've always known what I've got to live up to".

David also recognised that his disciplinary record would also come under scrutiny because of his dad; but said that "I've got a totally different style of play. The game's different to when he played; a totally different kettle of fish." Interviewed for this book, David said that one area he has not needed much advice on is disciplinary matters. In his professional career he has never been sent off, and his appearances at the Red Hall disciplinary committee have been few and far between: "When I did have to go once, Jim said not to tell them my surname" he recalls. Indeed, David's first suspension was in May 2013, as this book was being finished, after his part in a punch up at Batley when playing for Swinton. He says that Jim has told him to 'Count to three', but adds that Jim never got there!"

While playing for Widnes, David completed a sports science course. He played 93 games, scoring 8 tries. In 2006, he moved to London to play for Harlequins RL (now London Broncos) for two seasons, making 44 appearances and scoring two tries. He then moved to Humberside, and played two seasons for Hull KR; making 36 appearances and grabbing another two tries. In 2010 he returned to London for a further season at The Stoop, playing 14 more matches. Overall he played 187 Super League matches, scoring 12 tries. Subsequently he has played for Leigh Centurions in 2011, and was part of winning the Northern Rail Cup, and at the time of writing (May 2013) is playing his second season for Swinton Lions.

David says that the highlight of his career was "my first season at Widnes. I wasn't meant to be playing in the first game, against St Helens, but got in at the last minute." He kept his place, and established himself in the first team and Super League – "it all came at once" he reflected. Another memorable honour was playing for Lancashire: "I played in one of the 'Origin' matches, with people like Paul Sculthorpe and Andy Farrell. Also, I captained Wales against England at Doncaster in 2008. That was a massive privilege. We were well beaten, but Wales were going through a transitional phase with a lot of young players. But playing international rugby league, against the Australians and New Zealanders, is what every player aspires to do."

Another highlight of David's career was going on tour to Australia with the North West Counties under-18 team: "We went to Fiji and New Zealand, and had three and a half weeks in Australia and a couple of days in Los Angeles. That was a great experience."

David is now playing part-time with Swinton, and does groundwork, which he enjoys. If he stays in rugby when he retires, he says it will be in conditioning and developing weights programmes, rather than coaching.

Interviewed by Phil Caplan in *Rugby League World* in May 2008, he acknowledged Jim's influence. Asked if it was "galling to be constantly compared to your dad", he replied: I'm proud to follow in his footsteps. I ring him after every game and he's always giving me hints and tips, especially if there is something in my performance I`m not comfortable with." David also said that Jim "has also helped with contracts, and given advice about clubs as well. He has taken a massive interest in my career."

Any offspring of a famous sportsman, (or actor, painter, musician or politician for the matter) always carries the burden of comparison with their famous parent. David played for Swinton against Whitehaven in May 2013, a match broadcast live on Premier Sports. Despite it being over 33 years since Jim retired from playing, one of the commentators still mentioned that he is the son of "the great Jim Mills", an accolade David is happy to accept.

As well as club rugby league, David also played eight times for Wales, including captaining the side. He is actually an inch taller that his dad, and at his best playing weight slightly heavier that Jim at his peak. As outlined elsewhere, comparison between the two is of little value; they played in very different eras. But it is probably a relief to both his parents that David's career has been considerably less controversial than Jim's.

Jim says that "I am very proud of David, especially when he captained Wales. He had a lot to put up with following me and my reputation."

Jim is now 69 years old, and – apart from looking after a couple of houses he rents out and his after-dinner speaking to raise money for charity – is more or less retired. He still takes a great interest in rugby league, and regularly sees old playing colleagues and opponents at social events.

He enjoys life with Ruth, his children and grandchildren; and values their time in the sun in Spain. He can look back on a successful rugby league career, sometimes overshadowed by his disciplinary record, but nevertheless one that saw him play at the top level for 17 years, first in rugby union and then in rugby league. And at least now if he is heading along the M62 towards Leeds, it is usually for a social occasion or to watch a match, and not to try to explain to the disciplinary committee why he got his retaliation in first.

Appendix 1: Statistics and records

Compiled by Robert Gate and Peter Lush

Rugby Union

Welsh Youth XV	Opposition	Result
14 March 1963*	Welsh Secondary Schools XV	0–0
13 April 1963	Combined Midlands Colts XV	16–0
15 April 1963	English Schools XV	14–16
22 April 1963	French Juniors XV	0–9

* captain

Cardiff RFC First team	App	Tries
1963–64	6	1
1964–65	10	1
Totals	**16**	**2**

British club rugby league

	App	Sub	Tries
Halifax			
1965–66	5	0	0
1966–67	11	1	2
1967–68	21	0	4
Totals	**37**	**1**	**6**
Salford			
1967–68	4	1	0
Bradford Northern			
1968–69	19	2	3
1969–70	31	0	3
Totals	**50**	**2**	**6**
Widnes			
1972–73	22	0	5
1973–74	27	1	3
1974–75	35	0	5
1975–76	10	0	1
Totals	**94**	**1**	**14**
Workington Town			
1975–76	10	0	3
1976–77	13	0	0
Totals	**23**	**0**	**3**

Widnes

1976–77	14	0	4
1977–78	29	0	6
1978–79	34	0	13
1979–80	11	5	2
Totals	**88**	**5**	**21**

Australian club rugby league

	App	Tries
North Sydney		
1970	13	3
1971	17	4
1972	7	1
Totals	**37**	**8**

Representative rugby league

	App	Sub	Tries
Great Britain			
Test matches	6	0	0
Other matches	16	1	4
Wales			
International matches	17	0	3
Other matches	3	1	1
Other Nationalities	1	0	0
Totals	**43**	**2**	**8**

Career record

	App	Sub	Tries
Halifax	37	1	6
Salford	4	1	0
Bradford Northern	50	2	6
Widnes	182	6	39
Workington	23	0	3
North Sydney	37	0	8
Great Britain Tests	6	0	0
Wales internationals	17	0	3
1974 Great Britain other	12	1	2
1979 Great Britain other	4	0	2
1975 Wales other	3	1	1
Other Nationalities	1	0	0
Grand totals	**376**	**12**	**70**

Finals

Widnes

Challenge Cup
1974–75	Warrington	Won 14–7
1976–77	Leeds	Lost 16–7
1978–79	Wakefield Trinity	Won 12–3

John Player No.6 Trophy
1974–75	Bradford Northern	Lost 3–2
1975–76	Hull FC	Won 19–13
1978–79	Warrington	Won 16–4
1979–80	Bradford Northern	Lost 6–0

Lancashire Cup
1974–75	Salford	Won 6–2
1975–76	Salford	Won 16–7
1978–79	Workington Town	Won 15–13

Premiership
1977–78	Bradford Northern	Lost 17–8

BBC2 Floodlit Trophy
1972–73	Leigh	Lost 5–0
1978–79	St Helens	Won 13–7

Workington Town

Lancashire Cup
1976–77	Widnes	Lost 16–11

Test matches

Great Britain

15 June 1974	Australia	6–12	Brisbane	Blind side prop
6 July 1974	Australia	16–11	Sydney	Open side prop
4 Aug 1974	New Zealand	17–8	Christchurch	Open side prop
5 Nov 1978	Australia	18–14	Odsal	Open side prop
18 Nov 1978	Australia	6–23	Leeds	Open side prop
16 June 1979	Australia	0–35	Brisbane	Open side prop

Wales
(All at open side prop)

18 October 1969	England	23–40	Leeds	
23 October 1969	France	2–8	Salford	
25 January 1970	France	15–11	Perpignan	
24 February 1970	England	7–26	Leeds	
16 February 1975	France	21–8	Swansea	Try
25 February 1975	England	8–12	Salford	
1 0 June 1975 (WC)	England	12–7	Brisbane	
14 June 1975 (WC)	Australia	13––30	Sydney	
28 June 1975 (WC)	New Zealand	8–13	Auckland	Try
19 October 1975 (WC)	Australia	6–18	Swansea	
2 November 1975 (WC)	New Zealand	25–24	Swansea	
29 January 1977	England	6–2	Leeds	
20 February 1977	France	2–13	Toulouse	
15 January 1978	France	29–7	Widnes	Try
28 May 1978	England	13–60	St Helens	
15 October 1978	Australia	3–8	Swansea	
16 March 1979	England	7–15	Widnes	

Other tour matches

Great Britain

1974

26 May	Darwin	41–2	
2 June	Central Queensland	38–0	Sub (48 min)
4 June	Wide Bay	24–12	
9 June	Queensland	13–12	
20 June	North Coast	19–9	Try
23 June	Northern Division	38–14	
26 June	Western Division	25–10	
29 June	New South Wales	9–13	
30 June	Illawarra Division	26–22	
10 July	Riverina	36–10	
13 July	Newcastle	24–14	
1 August	Wellington	39–11	
6 August	South Island	33–2	

1979

25 May	North Queensland		
30 May	Wide Bay	Try	
8 June	Queensland	Try	
8 July	Monaro	Captain	

Wales

1975

5 June	Ipswich	35–13	Try
22 June	West Coast	35–5	
24 June	Canterbury	25–18	Sub
3 July	Maori	18–12	

Bibliography

Books
50 years of Welsh Youth Rugby 1949 – 1999, WYRU, n.d.
A Dream Come True, Doug Laughton with Andrew Quirke, London League Publications Ltd, 2003
Big Artie, Arthur Beetson with Ian Heads, ABC Books, 2004
Cardiff Rugby Club, D.E. Davies, Cardiff Athletic Club, 1975
Code Breaker, Jonathan Davies with Peter Corrigan, Bloomsbury, 1996
Glory Days, Alan Whiticker, New Holland Publishers, 2011
Gone North (Volume 1), Robert Gate, self-published, 1986
John Player Rugby League yearbooks 1973–74 to 1976–77, Jack Winstanley & Malcolm Ryding, Queen Anne Press
Legends of Australian Sport, Peter Meares, Penguin Books Australia, 2011
Made for Rugby, Barrie McDermott and Peter Smith, Sidgwick & Jackson, 2004
Merging on the ridiculous, Edited by Ian Clayton, Ian Daley & Brian Lewis, Yorkshire Arts Circus, 1995
Reilly, Malcolm Reilly with Harry Edgar, Mainstream Publishing, 1999
Rugby League in Twentieth Century Britain, Tony Collins, Routledge, 2006
Rugby League Lions, Robert Gate, Vertical Editions, 2008
Rugby League test matches in Australia, Alan Whiticker & Ian Collis, ABC Books, 1994
The History of Rugby League Clubs (second edition), Ian Collis & Alan Whiticker, New Holland, 2010
The Kangaroos, Ian Heads, Lester-Townsend Publishing, 1990
The Kiwis, John Coffey and Bernie Wood, Hodda Moa, 2007
The Mighty Bears!, Andrew Moore, Macmillan, 1996
The Premiership Clubs, Sean Fagan, RL1908.com, 2004
The Rugby League Challenge Cup, Les Hoole, Breedon Books, 1998
The Rugby League World Cup, League Publications, 2009
The Struggle for the Ashes II, Robert Gate, self-published, 1996
Those Who Played, Bruce Montgomerie, Montgomerie Publishing, 2004
To Jerusalem and Back, Simon Kelner, Macmillan, 1996
Tries in the Valleys, edited by Peter Lush & Dave Farrar, London League Publications Ltd, 1998
Wally Lewis, Adrian McGregor, University of Queensland Press, 2004

Magazines and newspapers
Daily Mirror
League Express
Open Rugby
Rugby League World
Rugby Leaguer
Western Mail
Widnes Weekly News

Various match programmes from rugby union and rugby league.

Other books from London League Publications Ltd:

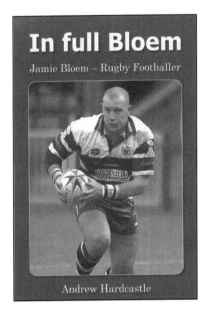

In full Bloem: The explosive biography of Jamie Bloem, current referee and former Halifax player. Published in February 2013 @ £14.95 (hardback), just £12.00 post free in the UK direct from London League Publications Ltd.

Heading for the line: Great new guidebook for rugby league grounds, published in April 2013 @ £7.95 (paperback), just £7.50 post free in the UK direct from London League Publications Ltd.

All our books can be ordered from any bookshop @ full price. To order direct from London League Publications Ltd visit our website: www.llpshop.co.uk or write to LLP, PO Box 65784, London NW2 9NS (cheques payable to London League Publications Ltd).

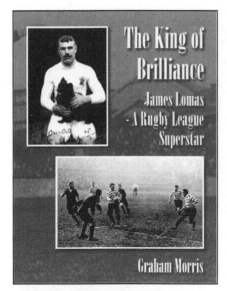

Great new book about one of the sport's genuine legends. James Lomas played for Bramley, Salford, Oldham and York, and won representative honours for Lancashire, Cumberland, England and Great Britain. He captained the first Lions team to tour Australia and New Zealand in 1910. This is the first biography of him.

Published in October 2011 at £16.95 (hardback). Special offer: £13.95 post free in the UK available direct from London League Publications Ltd, PO Box 65784, London NW2 9NS (cheques payable to London League Publications Ltd); credit card orders via our website: www.llpshop.co.uk or from any bookshop at full price.

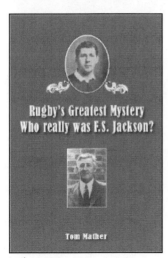

Rugby's Greatest Mystery
Who really was F.S. Jackson?

A true life rugby detective story
This is the story of a man whose life was made up of mystery, intrigue and deception, but was also a Rugby Union star before the First World War. He played for Leicester and Cornwall when they won the 1908 County Championship. He was selected for the Anglo-Welsh Rugby Union tour to New Zealand and Australia in 1908. However, the RFU recalled him from the tour and banned him from the sport over allegations that he was a professional player, and had played for Swinton in the Northern Union. The scandal around his suspension from rugby union caused great problems for the RFU and almost saw a further split in the game.

He then played Rugby League for New Zealand, against the British Lions in 1910. After the First World War he was reinstated by the New Zealand RU, became an East Coast selector and saw his son play for the All Blacks. For around 60 years he used the name Frederick Stanley Jackson, even though it was not his given name. When he died in 1957 he took to the grave his true identity. Even his family knew little about his early years in England, or even where he came from. **It was a mystery that remained unresolved until now.** The book also includes an analysis of the development of Leicester Tigers RFC up to the First World War.

Published in March 2012 at £12.95. Special offer £9.95 post free in the UK available direct from London League Publications Ltd, PO Box 65784, London NW2 9NS (cheques payable to London League Publications Ltd)
credit card orders via our website: www.llpshop.co.uk or from any bookshop.

Best in the Northern Union

The pioneering 1910
Rugby League Lions tour
of Australia and New Zealand

Tom Mather

Fascinating account of the first Great Britain Lions tour of Australia and New
Zealand. Published in 2010 at £12.95, special offer £10.00 post free in the UK
direct from London League Publications Ltd. Credit card orders via
www.llpshop.co.uk , orders by cheque to
LLP, PO Box 65784, London NW2 9NS

Braver than all the rest
A mother fights for her son

Philip Howard

Dave and Sarah Burgess are devastated when their young son Karl is found to have muscular dystrophy. Then another tragedy hits the family hard. But the family are committed to do the best they can for Karl, who has a passion for rugby league. Based in Castleton, a Yorkshire town near the border with Lancashire, Karl's determination to get the most out of life, despite his disability, inspires those around him, in particular Chris Anderton, one of the Castleton Rugby League Club players, who is coming to the end of his career in the game. A moving novel of family life and rugby league.
Published in 2010 at £9.95, special offer £7.00 post free in UK direct from London League Publications Ltd. Credit card orders via www.llpshop.co.uk , orders by cheque to LLP, PO Box 65784, London NW2 9NS

From grass
to glass

A Rugby League Journey

Paul Loughlin
with Andrew Quirke

Autobiography of Great Britain, St Helens, Huddersfield and Bradford Bulls Star.
Published in 2011 at £12.95, special offer £12.00 direct from London League
Publications Ltd. Credit card orders via www.llpshop.co.uk ,orders by cheque
to LLP, PO Box 65784, London NW2 9NS

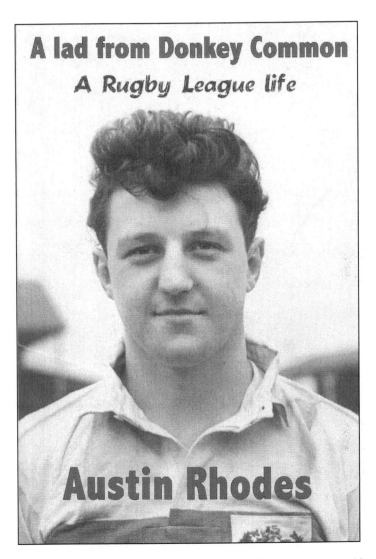

A lad from Donkey Common
A Rugby League life

Austin Rhodes

Austin Rhodes was virtually the complete player and his skills meant that he could cover several positions. Although several of his major triumphs were when playing at full-back, he was always a stand-off at heart.

His marvellous sporting story covers his early days at St Austin's school in Thatto Heath; his part in Saints' first-ever Challenge Cup success; Forces rugby union with the RAF; being a team-mate of Tom van Vollenhoven and further Championship and Challenge Cup glory in the late 1950s and early 1960s with St Helens. He was also a Rugby League World Cup winner with Great Britain. Spells at Leigh and Swinton are part of the story, along with a marvellous finale as coach of Pilkington Recs. Enjoy the fascinating story of a rugby league great.

Available from London League Publications Ltd for just £12.00 post free in the UK. Credit card orders via www.llpshop.co.uk; payment by cheque to PO Box 65784, London NW2 9NS. Available in bookshops at £12.95

Great new novel from Geoff Lee, his fifth about Ashurst in south east Lancashire. Available for just £9.00 post free in the UK direct from London League Publications Ltd. Credit card orders via www.llpshop.co.uk; payment by cheque to PO Box 65784, London NW2 9NS. Available in bookshops at £9.95.

Two of Geoff's previous novels, *One Winter* and *One Autumn,* are also available from London League Publications Ltd as above.

"Come on Northern"

The fall and rise of
Bradford Northern RLFC 1954 to 1965

Trevor Delaney

The collapse of Bradford Northern RLFC in December 1963 sent shock waves throughout rugby league in Great Britain. Northern were the first team to appear in three successive Wembley Cup finals, from 1947 to 1949, and were top of the league at the start of the 1954–55 season.

However, by December 1963, this once proud club had sunk to the bottom of the league table and withdrew from the competition in mid-season. It was the first time since the 1920s that a team had pulled out of the league without completing their fixtures. Their membership of the Rugby Football League was terminated and that season's record was expunged.

No club in the game's history had fallen from the heights quite like the old Northern. Their subsequent re-entry to the league was a great achievement for two men of vision – former Odsal greats, Trevor Foster and Joe Phillips.

The acclaimed rugby league historian, Trevor Delaney, recalls this period in the club's turbulent history. "*Come on Northern*" is an essential read for everyone interested in rugby league. Available for just £13.00 post free in the UK direct from London League Publications Ltd. Credit card orders via www.llpshop.co.uk; payment by cheque to PO Box 65784, London NW2 9NS. Available in bookshops at £13.95.

Many London League Publications Ltd books are now available as E-Books on Amazon.co.uk for Kindle readers. These can only be ordered from Amazon, not our website. These include some books that are not currently in print.

For all our books in print visit www.llpshop.co.uk or write to us at PO Box 65784, London NW2 9NS for a list of all our current titles.